Landbird Community Monitoring at Fort Sumter National Monument, 2010

Natural Resource Report NPS/SECN/NRDS—2011/303

Michael W. Byrne

USDI National Park Service
Southeast Coast Inventory and Monitoring Network
Cumberland Island National Seashore
101 Wheeler Street
Saint Marys, Georgia, 31558

Joe C. DeVivo

USDI National Park Service
Southeast Coast Inventory and Monitoring Network
University of Georgia
160 Phoenix Road, Phillips Lab
Athens, Georgia, 30605

and

Brent A. Blankley

USDI National Park Service
Southeast Coast Network
100 Alabama St SW
Atlanta, GA 30303

September 2011

U.S. Department of the Interior
National Park Service
Natural Resource Stewardship and Science
Fort Collins, Colorado

The National Park Service, Natural Resource Stewardship and Science office in Fort Collins, Colorado publishes a range of reports that address natural resource topics of interest and applicability to a broad audience in the National Park Service and others in natural resource management, including scientists, conservation and environmental constituencies, and the public.

The Natural Resource Data Series is intended for the timely release of basic data sets and data summaries. Care has been taken to assure accuracy of raw data values, but a thorough analysis and interpretation of the data has not been completed. Consequently, the initial analyses of data in this report are provisional and subject to change.

All manuscripts in the series receive the appropriate level of peer review to ensure that the information is scientifically credible, technically accurate, appropriately written for the intended audience, and designed and published in a professional manner. Data in this report were collected and analyzed using methods based on established, peer-reviewed protocols and were analyzed and interpreted within the guidelines of the protocols.

Views, statements, findings, conclusions, recommendations, and data in this report do not necessarily reflect views and policies of the National Park Service, U.S. Department of the Interior. Mention of trade names or commercial products does not constitute endorsement or recommendation for use by the U.S. Government.

This report is available from (http://science.nature.nps.gov/im/units/secn) and the Natural Resource Publications Management website (http://www.nature.nps.gov/publications/nrpm/).

Please cite this publication as:

NPS 392/110290, September 2011

Contents

Contents (continued)

Figures

Tables

Executive Summary

Birds are an important component of park ecosystems, and their high body temperature, rapid metabolism, and high ecological position in most food webs make them a good indicator of the effects of local and regional changes in ecosystems. Long-term trends in the community composition, relative abundance, distribution, and occurrences of breeding-bird populations provide a measure for assessing the ecological integrity and sustainability in southeastern systems. Further, long-term patterns of these attributes in relation to changes in the structural diversity of vegetation resulting from fire and other management practices will improve our understanding of the effects of various management actions. This report summarizes data collected with the Draft SECN Landbird Community Monitoring Protocol (Byrne et al., *in preparation*) at Fort Sumter National Monument in 2010.

1. Data were collected at five spatially-balanced random locations at the Monument using an adaptation of the variable-circular plot (VCP) technique with distance estimation.

2. Sampling activities occurred at the Monument in late April and again in late May in 2010.

3. We detected 200 birds representing 36 species; four of which were non-native species.

4. Monitoring efforts resulted in the addition of five new species to the Monument's official species list: green heron, chimney swift, Eastern kingbird, blue jay, and seaside sparrow.

5. Four non-native species were detected: Eurasian collared dove, European starling, house finch, house sparrow.

6. An evaluation of sampling effort relative to the number of species detected indicated that the sample adequately characterized the bird diversity, and analyses suggest bird diversity is moderate at the Monument.

7. Barn swallow, blue jay, boat-tailed grackle, Eurasian collared-dove, mourning dove, Northern cardinal, and Northern mockingbird were the most widely distributed species detected at the Monument.

8. The full dataset, and associated metadata, can be acquired from the data store at http://science.nature.nps.gov/nrdata/

.

Introduction

Overview

Birds are an important component of park ecosystems, and their high body temperature, rapid metabolism, and high ecological position in most food webs make them good indicators of the effects of local and regional changes in ecosystems. It has also been suggested that management activities aimed at preserving habitat for bird populations, such as for neotropical migrants, can have the added benefit of preserving entire ecosystems and their attendant ecosystem services (Karr 1991, Maurer and Heywood 1993). Moreover, birds have a tremendous following among the public, and many parks provide information on the status and trends of birds in their park through interpretive programs.

Bird populations are affected by a variety of stressors; however, the primary agents are habitat loss and degradation. The Southeastern U.S. has a long history of documented species extinctions associated with habitat loss, degradation, and over-harvest, including the passenger pigeon, Carolina parakeet, ivory-billed woodpecker, Zenaida dove, Key West quail-dove, and dusky seaside sparrow. Analysis of both Breeding Bird Survey and Christmas Bird Count (CBC) long-term datasets indicate decreasing counts and shifting and condensed ranges of many migratory and non-migratory bird species within the last 40 years (Sauer et al. 1997, Niven et al. 2009). The last four decades of CBC data indicate a northward shift in the occurrences of 68.2% (208/305) of the species detected (Niven et al. 2009). Although several factors are associated with changes in bird populations and ranges, climate change is suspected as a causative agent (Strode 2003, Butler 2003, Marra et al. 2005, Mills 2005, Murphy-Klassen et al. 2005, Visser and Both 2005); however habitat loss and degradation are the more likely agents in the short term. Bird communities are also good indicators of ecological conditions and several bioassessment approaches have been developed using birds (Croonquist and Brooks 1991, Bradford et al. 1998, O'Connell et al. 2000, Bryce et al. 2002, Coppedge et al. 2006).

The Southeastern U.S. serves as an important migration corridor and wintering ground for many northern-breeding species and as a breeding area for resident and breeding birds. All migratory species depend on quality stopover areas, and the juxtaposition of SECN parks in the Atlantic Flyway make them important stopover areas during the spring and fall migrations and also serve as key wintering areas for several species. The SECN has over 400 known bird species (NPSpecies 2011), including several state- and federally listed species. Consequently, birds ranked high in the SECN Vital Signs selection process.

Long-term trends in the community composition, diversity, and occupancy of breeding-bird populations provide a measure for assessing the ecological integrity and sustainability in southeastern systems, and identifying the need for specific management activities on our park lands. Further, long term trends in arrival phenology will assist park managers in developing and implementing mitigation strategies in response to predicted patterns in climate change.

The National Park Service Omnibus Management Act of 1998, and other reinforcing policies and regulations, require park managers "to establish baseline information and to provide information on the long-term trends in the condition of National Park System resources" (Title II, Sec. 204). The bird-community monitoring data summarized herein is a tool to assist park managers in fulfilling this mandate.

This report summarizes data collected under the draft SECN Landbird Community Monitoring Protocol (Byrne et al., *in preparation*).

Study Area

Fort Sumter National Monument (FOSU) is in Charleston, South Carolina (Figure 1) within the mouth of the Charleston Harbor and on the southern tip of Sullivan's Island. The Monument is co-administered with Charles Pinckney National Historic Site (CHPI), although CHPI was not included as part of these monitoring efforts. The Monument is 81-ha (200 ac), of which approximately 50 ha (122 ac) is submerged in the Harbor. Although the Monument is primarily managed as an important cultural site (i.e., it was the site of the first engagement of the Civil War), it also contains natural resources. These resources provide important stop-over sites for migratory birds, and an accreted area adjacent to the fort and the beachfront areas on Sullivan's Island provides foraging habitat for shorebirds year-round.

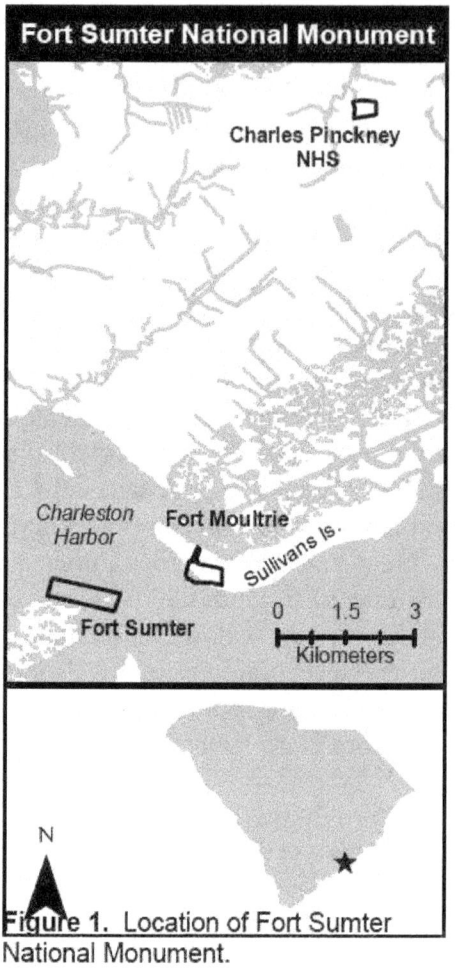

Figure 1. Location of Fort Sumter National Monument.

Vegetation is sparse around the fort itself, and consists primarily of early-successional tidal forbs (e.g., *Batis maritima*). The vegetation communities in the unit on Sullivan's Island are somewhat more complex, although impacted from strong anthropogenic use, and consist of primary dune, beach, and maritime hammock communities, and manicured lawn areas. The primary dune is characterized by sea oats (*Uniola paniculata*), while the maritime hammock is dominated by Virginia live oak (*Quercus virginiana*).

Dredging activities within the Harbor pose a potential threat to the source of sand, and other material, for the accreted area adjacent to the fort, although dredging activities are closely monitored by park managers.

FOSU has 183 known bird species, including five species added to the park's species list as a result of this monitoring effort (Appendix A).

Sampling Period Climate Conditions

Climatologically, the Southeastern U.S. experienced cooler than normal average temperatures during much of 2010. Winter minimum temperatures were up to 10°F below normal during December 2010. Based on data collected within 13 km (8 mi) of FOSU, mean monthly temperatures were approximately normal during the period when landbird monitoring occurred, (Figure 2), ranging from 66.9°F to 75.5°F during April and May (Wright et al. 2011). Precipitation during the sampling period was well below average during April (i.e., 20% of the average) and just above average in May. Precipitation during the two months prior to monitoring were approximately average and the preceding winter season was slightly wetter than average (Figure 3).

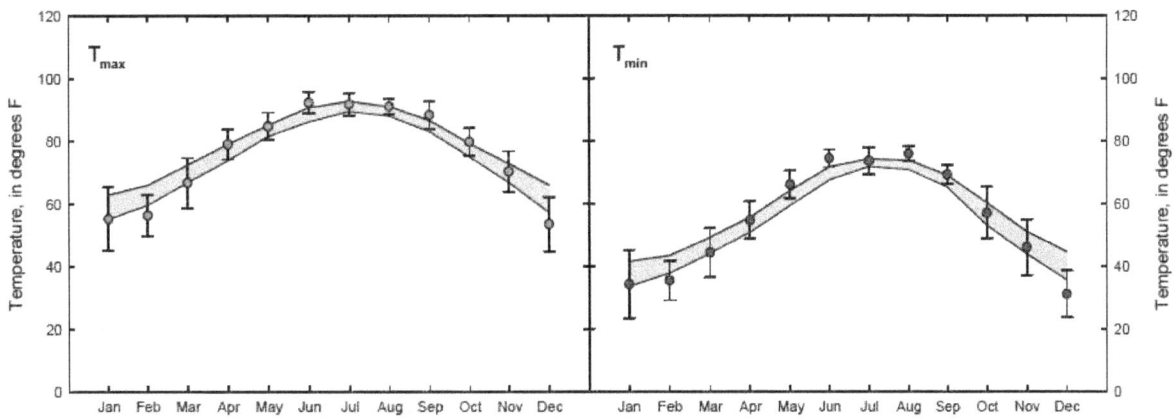

Figure 2. 2010 temperature departures from 30-year (1981 - 2010) average for Charleston International Airport station, 13 km from FOSU. Depicted in this graph are average maximum monthly temperature (T_{max}) and average minimum monthly temperature (T_{min}). Gray shaded region represents 30-year average and standard deviation. Error bars represent standard deviation of T_{max} and T_{min} during 2010.

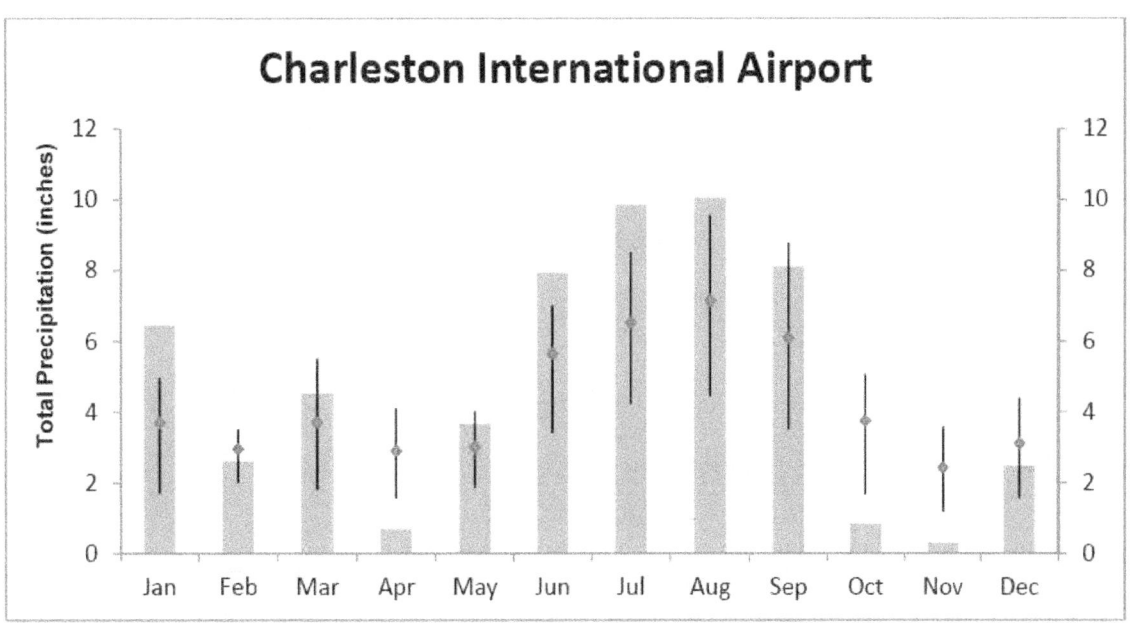

Figure 3. 2010 precipitation departures from 30-year (1981 - 2010) average for Charleston International Airport station, 13km from FOSU. Gray bars indicate 2010 precipitation totals for each month and error bars represent the normal (dots), 25th, and 75th percentile for the 30-year average.

Monitoring Objective

- Determine trends in landbird-species occupancy, distribution, diversity, and community composition in SECN parks.

Methods

Sampling Design

A detailed explanation of the sampling design and site selection can be found in the SECN Draft Landbird Monitoring Protocol (Byrne et al., *in preparation*) and sample site selection SOP (Byrne 2009). In summary, to allow for park-wide inference, the FOSU administrative boundary was used as the sampling frame. The sampling frame was divided into a systematic 0.5-ha grid; the center point of each grid cell served as the potential sampling site. A spatially-balanced sample was drawn from this grid using the Reversed Randomized Quadrant-Recursive Raster (RRQRR) algorithm (Theobald et al. 2007). Alternate points were used when selection criteria (i.e., including safety and access issues) were not met. A sample size of five was chosen after consideration of the Monument's size, hypothesized variability, and logistical issues (Figure 4).

Sampling Methodology

We used an adaptation of variable-circular plot (VCP) technique with distance estimation (Reynolds et al. 1980, Ralph et al. 1993, Fancy 1997, Buckland et al. 1993, 2001). Bird surveys were conducted at the center point of each 0.5-ha macroplot (see Sampling Design) from April – June. This time period was selected to maximize detecting species that reproduce within the parks and also detect migratory birds. All birds observed by sight and sound were recorded. Surveys occurred from 0530 – 1100. Upon arrival at the station, all sampling event information was recorded. Sampling began five to ten minutes after arriving at the sample location to allow birds present to resume normal behaviors. Data were not collected at Beaufort wind speed codes greater than 6 (i.e., winds >24mph), as this substantially impedes detectability.

At each station, counts were separated into four time segments of equal duration, 0-3 minutes (to allow comparisons with BBS data), 3-6 minutes, 5-9 minutes, and 9-12 minutes. Distance to each bird detected was estimated and categorized into one of four distance classes (0-25 m, 25-50, 50-100, >100). Birds considered flyovers were also recorded. Each sampling location was sampled two times during the sampling period, at least three weeks apart, in an effort to detect migrants or breeders that arrive at different times of the year. All detections were made via auditory cues or visual observations with binoculars.

Data Analysis

Data in this report represent one year and are summarized in three general categories: diversity, composition, and distribution. Sampling locations are presented in Figure 4, labeled locations are presented in Appendix B, and species detected at each location are presented in Appendix C. Despite a well-trained and dedicated field crew, complete identification of all individuals encountered was not always possible. Species were identified to the most refined taxonomic level possible (e.g., *Corvus*, Parulidae, Ciconiiformes).

Composition

Measures of community composition are often good indicators of abiotic variability, disturbance, or other stressors. Summaries related to sample composition include the total number of individuals and species detected, and proportional abundances of each species in the overall sample. For all species detected we calculated the proportion of sites where the species was detected at least once. All non-native species detections were pooled to calculate the proportion of sites where at least one non-native species was detected. Summaries of composition are presented for all landbirds detected. This section also presents any new species detected and addresses the detection of any species of management concern or interest.

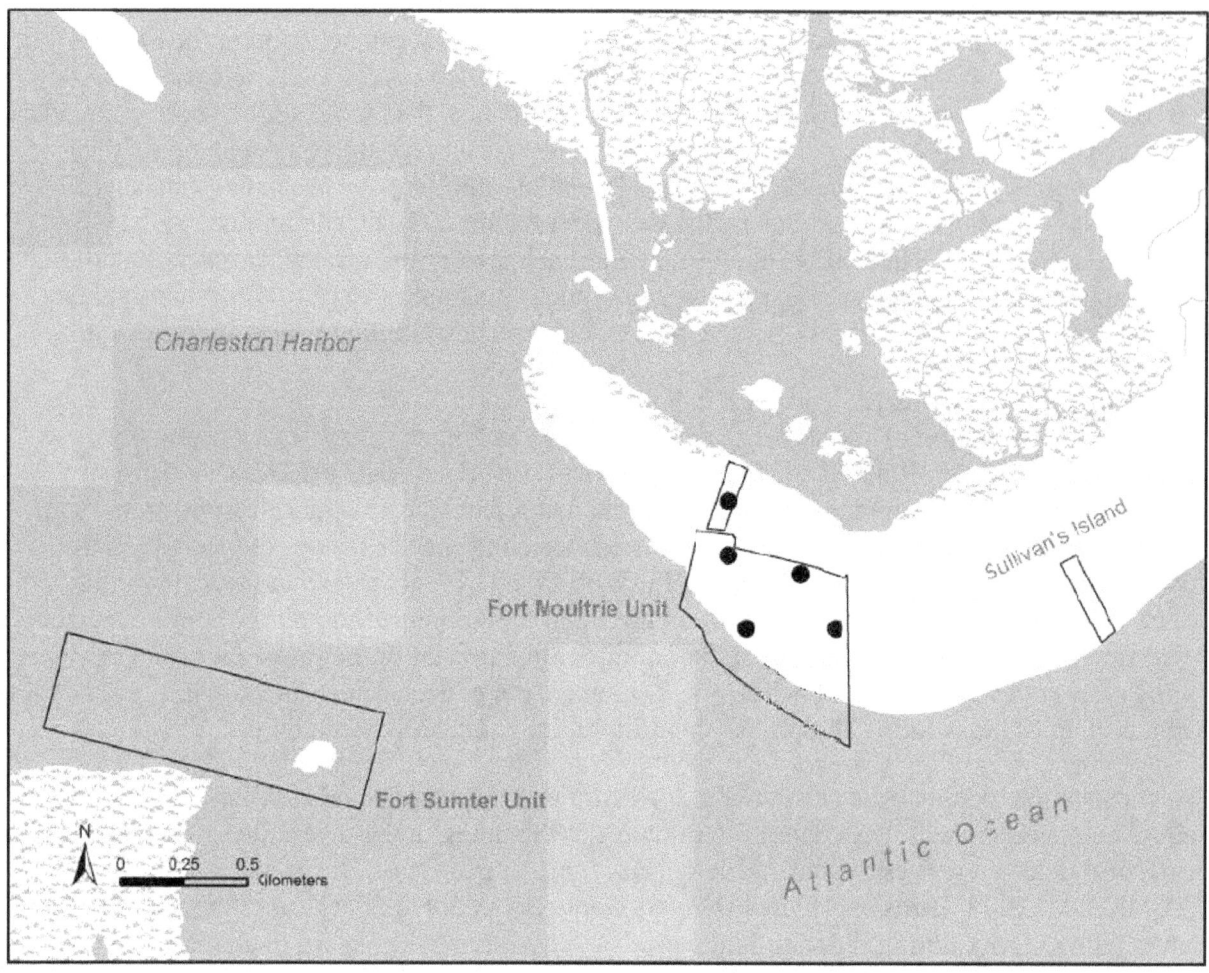

Figure 4. Spatially-balanced random sampling locations at Fort Sumter National Monument, 2010.

Distribution
Understanding changes in the distribution of bird species is integral to informed management of species and their requisite habitats. Changes in species distributions over time provide useful information at both the local and landscape scale relating to how species respond to large-scale influences such as changing land use, climate, hydrology, or habitat quality/ availability. Climate change, for example, influences the distribution, phenology, population demographics, and abundance of individual bird species. Cascading effects through altered species interactions and alterations within the web structure will also have the capacity to impact ecosystem processes (Montoya and Raffaelli 2010, USGS 2011).

Diversity
Diversity is defined as "the variety and abundance of species in a defined unit of study" (Magurran 2004, p. 3). Diversity is a community property that is related to trophic structure, productivity, stability, (McIntosh 1967, McNaughton 1977), immigration / emigration (Colwell and Lee 2000), and ecological condition (i.e., ecological integrity as defined by Karr and Chu

1995). Species diversity consists of two components: the number of species (species richness) and the relative abundance of those species (species evenness / dominance) within a defined community (Margalef 1958, Lloyd and Ghelardi 1964, Pielou 1966). Species diversity is often communicated in the form of diversity indices. The term community refers to the assemblage of species populations that occur together in space and time (Begon et al. 1986), and we consider the Monument as a whole community as per the conceptual ecological models presented in our monitoring plan (see Chapter 2 in DeVivo et al. 2008).

Because diversity indices respond differently to various mechanisms that influence community change, several indices must be used to adequately characterize diversity in SECN parks (Haedrick 1975, Boyle et al. 1984). After careful appraisal of advantages and disadvantages of the many diversity indices, a suite of alpha diversity indices were selected to summarize these data (Table 1), where alpha diversity is the diversity of species within a defined area, community, or ecosystem (Whittaker 1972).

Species diversity estimates are based only on bird observations identified to the species level, as they were the primary target of this monitoring effort. Non-native birds were not included in diversity estimates.

Table 1. Diversity indices used, corresponding symbol, community attribute the index reflects, the range of index values, and notes on each index.

Index	Symbol	Community Attribute	Index Citation	Notes
Native Spp. Richness	S_{obs}	Richness	n/a	Value is a positive integer that indicates the number of native species in the sample. Intuitive. Good discriminant ability if sampling effort is comparable; sensitive to sample size, the occurrence of rare species, or those with low detectability; does not account for relative abundances.
Chao 1	**Chao1**	Richness	Chao (1984) Chao (1987)	Values indicate an estimate of species richness; abundance-based estimate; works well with dataset containing several infrequent observations[a].
Chao 2	**Chao2**	Richness	Chao (1984) Chao (1987)	Values indicate an estimate of total species richness (including species not present in the sample); incidence-based estimate; works well with dataset containing several infrequent observations[a].
Abundance-based Coverage	**ACE**	Richness	Chao and Lee (1992) Chazdon et al. (1998)	Values indicate an estimate of species richness; abundance-based estimate.
Incidence-based Coverage	**ICE**	Richness	Lee and Chao (1994) Chazdon et al. (1998)	Values indicate an estimate of total species richness (including species not present in the sample); incidence-based estimate.
Jackknife 1	**Jack1**	Richness	Burnham and Overton (1978) Burnham and Overton (1979) Heltshe and Forrester (1983)	Values indicate an estimate of total species richness (including species not present in the sample); incidence-based estimate; The higher the value the higher the species richness. This procedure requires no assumptions regarding the data distribution.
Jackknife 2	**Jack2**	Richness	Smith and van Belle (1984)	Values indicate an estimate of species richness; incidence-based estimate.
Bootstrap	**Boot**	Richness	Smith and van Belle (1984)	Values indicate an estimate of species richness; incidence-based estimate.

[a] (Chao 1984), [b] (Kempton 2002), [c] (Kempton and Taylor 1974), [d] (Hayek and Buzas 1997), [e] (Wolda 1983), [f] (Kempton and Wedderburn 1978), [g] (Magurran 1988), [h] (Lexerød and Eid 2006), [i] (Magurran 2004)

Table 1. Continued.

Index	Symbol	Community Attribute	Index Citation	Notes
Fisher's α	α	Richness	Fisher et al. (1943)	Value is a positive integer and indicates a relative estimate of species richness; good discriminant ability, low sensitivity to sample size, and robust to deviations in the assumed distribution [b, c, d, e]; abundance-based estimate.
Q Statistic	Q	Richness	Kempton and Taylor (1976) Kempton and Taylor (1978)	Value is a positive integer and indicates a relative estimate of species richness. Good discriminant ability and low bias with small samples[f], model fit is irrelevant to index performance[g]; value is not weighted towards abundant or rare species; abundance-based estimate.
Smith and Wilson	E_{var}	Evenness	Smith and Wilson (1996)	Values range from 0 (no evenness) to 1 (perfectly even and all species exists in relatively equal abundance); weighs common species more heavily than rare species (desirable in certain cases).
Smith and Wilson 1/D	$E_{1/D}$	Evenness	Smith and Wilson (1996) Simpson (1949)	Values range from 0 (no evenness) to 1 (perfectly even and all species exists in relatively equal abundance); weighs rare and abundant species equally (desirable in certain cases).
Camargo	E'	Evenness	Camargo (1992)	Values range from 0 (no evenness) to 1 (perfectly even and all species exists in relatively equal abundance); performs well estimating intermediate values of evenness than the other indices; weighs rare and abundant species equally (desirable in certain cases).
Gini	E_G	Evenness	Gini (1912)	Values range from 0 (no evenness) to 1 (perfectly even and all species exists in relatively equal abundance); Good discriminant ability and low sensitivity to sample size[h].
Berger-Parker	D_{BP}	Dominance	Berger and Parker (1970)	Values range from 0 (no single-species dominance) to 1 (sample is strongly dominated by a single species; describes the proportional dominance of the single most abundant species; low sensitivity to sample size but poor discriminant ability[j] – not used for across year or site comparisons.

[a] (Chao 1984), [b] (Kempton 2002), [c] (Kempton and Taylor 1974), [d] (Hayek and Buzas 1997), [e] (Wolda 1983), [f] (Kempton and Taylor 1976), [h] (Lexerød and Eid 2006), [i] (Magurran 2004)
[g] (Magurran 1988), [h] (Kempton and Wedderburn 1978),

Results

Composition

We detected 200 birds representing 36 species. The majority of the sample consisted of boat-tailed grackle (14%), followed by Northern mockingbird (7.5%), blue jay (7.5%), and brown pelican (7.5%) (Figure 5). Occupancy provides insight into the distribution of species across the park and whether a species is commonly or uncommonly encountered; however, this is strongly influenced by a species' detectability (which is affected by habitat characteristics and will be accounted for in future analyses) as more-easily detected species can be more frequently encountered. Barn swallow, blue jay, boat-tailed grackle, Eurasian collared-dove, mourning dove, Northern cardinal, and Northern mockingbird occurred at all sampling locations (Table 2). Four non-native species were detected: Eurasian collared dove, European starling, house finch, and house sparrow.

Several species identified by Watson and Malloy (2008) as priority species were detected during this sampling effort, including: brown pelican, chimney swift, Eastern kingbird, least tern, painted bunting, prothonotary warbler, royal tern, seaside sparrow, semipalmated sandpiper, white-eyed vireo, and white-throated sparrow.

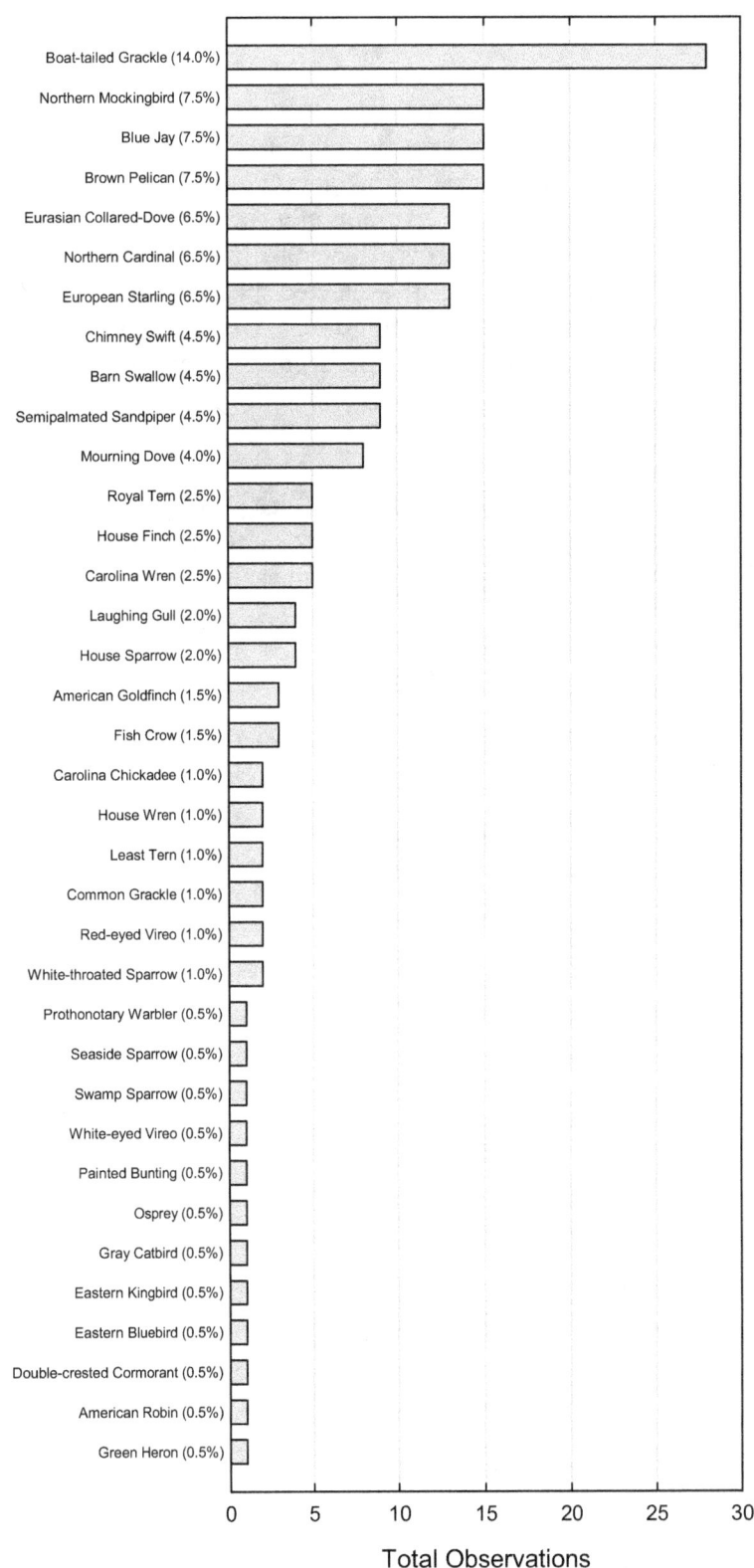

Figure 5. Proportions of bird species observed at Fort Sumter National Monument, 2010.

Table 2. Proportion of sites where each bird species was detected at Fort Sumter National Monument, 2010.

Common Name	Scientific Name	Proportion of Sites Where Observed
Barn Swallow	*Hirundo rustica*	1.00
Blue Jay	*Cyanocitta cristata*	1.00
Boat-tailed Grackle	*Quiscalus major*	1.00
Eurasian Collared-Dove	*Streptopelia decaocto*	1.00
Mourning Dove	*Zenaida macroura*	1.00
Northern Cardinal	*Cardinalis cardinalis*	1.00
Northern Mockingbird	*Mimus polyglottos*	1.00
Brown Pelican	*Pelecanus occidentalis*	0.80
Chimney Swift	*Chaetura pelagica*	0.80
House Finch	*Carpodacus mexicanus*	0.80
Royal Tern	*Sterna maxima*	0.80
American Goldfinch	*Carduelis tristis*	0.60
Carolina Wren	*Thryothorus ludovicianus*	0.60
European Starling	*Sturnus vulgaris*	0.60
House Sparrow	*Passer domesticus*	0.60
Laughing Gull	*Larus atricilla*	0.60
Carolina Chickadee	*Poecile carolinensis*	0.40
Fish Crow	*Corvus ossifragus*	0.40
House Wren	*Troglodytes aedon*	0.40
Least Tern	*Sterna antillarum*	0.40
White-throated Sparrow	*Zonotrichia albicollis*	0.40
American Robin	*Turdus migratorius*	0.20
Common Grackle	*Quiscalus quiscula*	0.20
Double-crested Cormorant	*Phalacrocorax auritus*	0.20
Eastern Bluebird	*Sialia sialis*	0.20
Eastern Kingbird	*Tyrannus tyrannus*	0.20
Gray Catbird	*Dumetella carolinensis*	0.20
Green Heron	*Butorides virescens*	0.20
Osprey	*Pandion haliaetus*	0.20
Painted Bunting	*Passerina ciris*	0.20
Prothonotary Warbler	*Protonotaria citrea*	0.20
Red-eyed Vireo	*Vireo olivaceus*	0.20
Seaside Sparrow	*Ammodramus maritimus*	0.20
Semipalmated Sandpiper	*Calidris pusilla*	0.20
Swamp Sparrow	*Melospiza georgiana*	0.20
White-eyed Vireo	*Vireo griseus*	0.20

New Species Records

Five new bird species were added to the FOSU species list as a result of the 2010 monitoring efforts (Table 3): green heron, chimney swift, Eastern kingbird, blue jay, and seaside sparrow.

Table 3. New bird species detected at Fort Sumter National Monument and recommended NPSpecies classifications.

Common Name(s)	Abundance	Residency	Nativity	Pest	Management Priority	Exploitation Concerns
Green Heron	Rare	Breeder	Native	No	No	No
Chimney Swift	Uncommon	Breeder	Native	No	No	No
Eastern Kingbird	Rare	Breeder	Native	No	No	No
Blue Jay	Common	Breeder	Native	No	No	No
Seaside Sparrow	Rare	Breeder	Native	No	No	No

Distribution

Barn swallow, blue jay, boat-tailed grackle, Eurasian collared-dove, mourning dove, Northern cardinal, and Northern mockingbird were the most widely distributed species at the Monument, occurring at all sampling locations (Appendix D). Brown pelican, chimney swift, house finch, and royal tern were detected at 80% of the sampling locations (Appendix D).

Appendix D contains distribution maps for all species detected during surveys. The sampling locations where each species was detected and was not detected are depicted on each map.

Diversity

Diversity indices calculated for these data were selected to reflect community composition (i.e., number of species) and structure (i.e., number of individuals), which include species richness and evenness estimates (Table 4). Confidence intervals for each diversity index were estimated with a bootstrap procedure. A brief explanation of interpreting the value is presented in Table 2.

Rank-abundance plots, frequency distributions, and other descriptive approaches were used to explore the abundance distributions and patterns in the dataset, and evaluate the utility of select indices and abundance equitability among species. The data are best fit by a log-series abundance model; χ^2=3.6888, df=3, p=0.2971. The dispersion (i.e., the variance / mean) also suggests that species are not aggregated and occur uniformly across the Monument.

The species accumulation curve generated from the data asymptotes at exactly five samples (i.e., equal to the total number of samples collected), validating the sample size as effective in characterizing bird diversity at the Monument.

Observed native-species richness (i.e., S_{obs}) was 32 (95% CI: 25.16, 38.83). Species-richness estimators are relatively consistent and range from 36.93 – 49.80 (Table 3). Because of the uncertainty associated with the Chao estimators (as indicated by the high confidence intervals) due to the characteristics of the dataset, the ACE, ICE, Jack1, Jack2, and Boot richness estimators are likely better estimates of true species richness. Diversity indices suggest medium bird-species diversity at the Monument (α=11.83, Q=8.87; Table 3). The sample was relatively well distributed among species, with seven species accounting for 56% of the sample (Figure 5).

Evenness/dominance indices (i.e., E_{var}, $E_{1/D}$, E_g, E', and D_{BP}) are consistent suggesting varied relative abundances of the species in the sample and a compositionally diverse bird community at the Monument. Because 2010 monitoring efforts were the first for this vital sign at the Monument, these values will serve as a baseline for comparison with future monitoring efforts.

Table 4. Bird alpha-diversity estimates at Fort Sumter National Monument, 2010.

Index	Symbol	Value	Lower 95% CI	Upper 95% CI	Value Interpretation
Native Spp. Richness	S_{obs}	32.00	25.16	38.83	Number of native species detected
Chao 1	Chao1	44.10	35.03	88.28	Estimated true species richness (high CI)
Chao 2	Chao2	56.50	38.52	123.93	Estimated true species richness (high CI)
Abundance-based Coverage	ACE	43.43	32.32	54.54	Estimated true species richness
Incidence-based Coverage	ICE	47.62	37.49	57.75	Estimated true species richness
Jackknife 1	Jack1	43.20	36.03	50.37	Estimated true species richness
Jackknife 2	Jack2	49.80	41.63	57.97	Estimated true species richness
Bootstrap	Boot	36.93	32.72	41.14	Estimated true species richness
Fisher's α	α	11.83	9.13	14.53	Baseline value, suggests high diversity
Q Statistic	Q	8.87	5.86	10.78	Baseline value, suggests medium diversity
Smith and Wilson	E_{var}	0.47	0.42	0.57	Species occur in several relative abundances –medium evenness
Smith and Wilson 1/D	$E_{1/D}$	0.45	0.40	0.60	Species occur in several relative abundances –medium evenness
Camargo	E'	0.79	0.73	0.93	Species in the middle of the distribution occur in few relative abundances – high evenness
Gini	E_G	0.44	0.29	0.59	Species occur in several relative abundances –medium evenness
Berger-Parker	D_{BP}	0.17	0.12	0.22	Sample is not dominated by a single species, diverse assemblage

Literature Cited

Begon, M., J. L. Harper, and C. R. Townsend. 1986. Ecology: Individuals, populations and communities. Blackwell Scientific, Oxford, UK.

Berger, W. H., and F. L. Parker. 1970. Diversity of planktonic foraminifera in deep-sea sediments. Science 168:1345-1347.

Boyle, T. P., J. Sebaugh, and E. Robinson-Wilson. 1984. A hierarchical approach to the measurement of changes in community structure induced by environmental stress. Journal of Testing and Evaluation 12:241-245.

Bradford, D. F., S. E. Franson, A. C. Neale, D. T. Heggem, G. R. Miller, and G. E. Canterbury. 1998. Bird species assemblages as indicators of biological integrity in Great Basin rangeland. Environmental Monitoring and Assessment 49:1–22.

Bryce, S. A., R. M. Hughes, and P. R. Kaufmann. 2002. Development of a bird integrity index: Using bird assemblages as indicators of riparian condition. Environmental Management 30:294-310.

Buckland, S. T., D. R. Anderson, K. P. Burnham, and J. L. Laake. 1993. Distance Sampling: Estimating Abundance of Biological Populations. Chapman and Hall, New York.

Buckland, S. T., D. R. Anderson, K. P. Burnham, J. L. Laake, D. L. Borchers, and L. Thomas. 2001. Introduction to distance sampling: Estimating abundance of biological populations. Oxford University Press. 432 pp.

Burnham, K. P., and W. S. Overton. 1978. Estimation of the size of a closed population when capture probabilities vary among animals. Biometrika 65:623-633.

Burnham, K. P., and W. S. Overton. 1979. Robust estimation of population size when capture probabilities vary among animals. Ecology 60:927-936.

Butler, C. J. 2003. The disproportionate effect of global warming on the arrival dates of short-distant migratory birds in North America. Ibis 145:484-495.

Byrne, M. W. 2009. Sampling-point generation for SECN monitoring protocols: Generating a spatially-balanced random sample with the RRQRR tool in ArcGIS 9.1. Draft Standard Operating Procedure Version 1.0, last updated March 2009.

Byrne, M. W., B. D. Smrekar, C. J. Wright, and E. Thompson. *In preparation*. Draft bird community monitoring in Southeast Coast Network parks. USDI National Park Service, Southeast Coast Network, Atlanta, GA, USA.

Camargo, J. A. 1992. New diversity index for assessing structural alterations in aquatic communities. Bulletin of Environmental Contamination and Toxicology 48:428-434.

Chao, A. 1984. Non-parametric estimation of the number of classes in a population. Scandinavian Journal of Statistics 11:265-270.

Chao, A. 1987. Estimating the population size for capture-recapture data with unequal catchability. Biometrics 43:783-791.

Chao, A., and S. M Lee. 1992. Estimating the number of classes via sample coverage. Journal of the American Statistical Association 87:210-217.

Chazdon, R. L., R. K. Colwell, J. S. Denslow, and M. R. Guariguata. 1998. Statistical methods for estimating species richness of woody regeneration in primary and secondary rain forests of NE Costa Rica. Pp. 285-309 *in* F. Dallmeier and J. A. Comiskey, eds., Forest biodiversity research, monitoring and modeling: Conceptual background and Old World case studies. Parthenon Publishing, Paris, FR.

Colwell, R. K., and D. C. Lees. 2000. The mid-domain effect: Geometric constraints on the geography of species richness. Trends in Ecology and Evolution 15:70–76.

Coppedge, B. R., D. M. Engle, R. E. Masters, and M.S. Gregory. 2006. Development of a grassland index based on breeding bird assemblages. Environmental Monitoring and Assessment 118:125–145.

Croonquist, M. J., and R. P. Brooks. 1991. Use of avian and mammalian guilds as indicators of cumulative impacts in riparian-wetland areas. Environmental Management 15:701-714.

DeVivo, J. C., C. J. Wright, M. W. Byrne, E. DiDonato, and T. Curtis. 2008. Vital signs monitoring in the Southeast Coast Inventory & Monitoring Network. Natural Resource Report NPS/SECN/NRR—2008/061. National Park Service, Fort Collins, CO, USA.

Fancy, S. G. 1997. A new approach for analyzing bird densities from variable circular-plot counts. Pacific Science 51:107-114.

Fisher, R. A., A. S. Corbet, and C. B. Williams. 1943. The relation between the number of species and the number of individuals in a random sample of animal population. Journal of Animal Ecology 12:42–58.

Gini, C. 1912. Measurement of inequality on income. Economic Journal 31:22-43.

Haedrick, R. 1975. Diversity and overlap as measures of environmental quality. Water Research 9:945–949.

Hayek, L. A., and M. A. Buzas. 1997. Surveying natural populations. Columbia University Press, New York, USA.

Heltshe, J., and N. E. Forrester. 1983. Estimating species richness using the jackknife procedure. Biometrics 39:1-11.

Karr, J. R. 1991. Biological integrity: a long-neglected aspect of water resource management. Ecological Applications 1:66–84.

Karr, J. R., and E. W. Chu. 1995. Ecological integrity: Reclaiming lost connections. Pp. 34-48 *in* Westra, L., and J. Lemons (eds.), Perspective on ecological integrity. Kluwer Academic Publishing, NL.

Kempton, R. A., and L. R. Taylor. 1974. Log-series and log-normal parameters as diversity discriminants for the Lepidoptera. Journal of Animal Ecology 43:381–399.

Kempton, R. A., and L. R. Taylor. 1976. Models and statistics for species diversity. Nature 262:818–820.

Kempton, R. A., and L. R. Taylor. 1978. The Q-statistic and the diversity of floras. Nature 275:252-253.

Kempton, R. A., and R. W. M. Wedderburn. 1978. A comparison of three measures of species diversity. Biometrics 34:22-37.

Kempton, R. A. 2002. Species diversity. Encyclopedia of Environmetrics 4:2086-2092.

Lee, S. M., and A. Chao. 1994. Estimating population size via sample coverage for closed capture-recapture models. Biometrics 50:88-97.

Lexerød, N. L., and T. Eid. 2006. An evaluation of different diameter diversity indices based on criteria related to forest management planning. Forest Ecology and Management 222:17–28.

Lloyd, M., and R. J. Ghelardi. 1964. A table for calculating the "equitability" component of species diversity. Journal of Animal Ecology 33:217-225.

MacKenzie, D. I., J. D. Nichols, G. B. Lachman, S. Droege, J. A. Royle, and C. A. Langtimm. 2002. Estimating site occupancy when detection probabilities are less than one. Ecology 83:2248–2255.

Magurran, A. E. 1988. Ecological diversity and its measurement. Cambridge University Press, Cambridge, UK.

Magurran, A. E. 2004. Measuring biological diversity. Blackwell Publishing, Oxford, UK.

Margalef, D. R. 1958. Information theory in ecology. General Systems 3: 36-71.

Marra, P. P., C. M. Francis, R. S. Mulvihill, and F .R. Moore. 2005. The influence of climate on the timing and rate of spring bird migration. Oecologia 142: 307-315.

Maurer, B. A., and S. G. Heywood. 1993. Geographic range fragmentation and abundance in neotropical migratory birds. Conservation Biology 7:501-509.

McIntosh, R. I. 1967. An index of diversity and the relation of certain concepts to diversity. Ecology 48:392–404.

McNaughton, S. J. 1977. Diversity and stability of ecological communities: a comment on the role of empiricism in ecology. American Naturalist 111:515–525.

Montoya, J. M., and D. Raffaelli. 2010. Climate change, biotic interactions and ecosystem services. Philosophical Transactions of the Royal Society B 365: 2013–2018.

Mills, A. M. 2005. Changes in the timing of spring and autumn migration in North American migrant passerines during a period of global warming. Ibis 147: 259-260.

Murphy-Klassen H. M., T. J. Underwood, S. G. Sealy, and A. A. Czyrnyj. 2005. Long-term trends in spring arrival dates of migrant birds at Delta Marsh, Manitoba in relation to climate change. Auk 122:1130-1148.

Niven, D. K., G. S. Butcher, and G. T. Bancroft. 2009. Christmas bird counts and climate change: Northward shifts in early winter abundance. American Birds 82:10-15. Available online: http://web4.audubon.org/bird/cbc/pdf/AB_109_CBC_and_Climate_Change.pdf.

NPSpecies - The National Park Service Biodiversity Database. Secure online version. https://science1.nature.nps.gov/npspecies/web/main/start (Park list: accessed 1/13/2011).

O'Connell, T. L., L. E. Jackson, and R. P. Brooks. 2000. Bird guilds as indicators of ecological condition in the central Appalachians. Ecological Application 10:1706–1721.

Pielou, E. C. 1966. Species-diversity and pattern-diversity in the study of ecological succession. Journal of Theoretical Biology 10:370-383.

Ralph, C. J., G. R. Geupel, P. Pyle, T. E. Martin, and D. F. DeSante. 1993. Handbook of field methods for monitoring birds. General technical Report PSW-GTR-144-www. USDI Forest Service, Pacific Southwest Research Station, Albany, CA. 41 pp.

Reynolds, R. T., J. M. Scott, and R. A. Nussbaum. 1980. A variable circular-plot method for estimating bird numbers. Condor 82:309-313.

Sauer J. R., J. E. Hines, G. Hough, I. Thomas, and B. G. Peterjohn. 1997. The North American Breeding bird Survey Results and Analysis. Version 96.4. Patuxent Wildlife Research Center. Laurel, Maryland.

Simpson, E. H. 1949. Measurement of diversity. Nature 163:688.

Smith, B., and J. B. Wilson. 1996. A consumer's guide to evenness measures. Oikos 76:70-82.

Smith, E. P. and G. van Belle. 1984. Nonparametric estimation of species richness. Biometrics 40:119-129.

Strode, P. K. 2003. Implications of climate change for North American wood warblers (Parulidae). Global Change Biology 9:1137-1144.

Theobald, D. M., D. L. Stevens, D. White, N. S. Urquhart, A. R. Olsen, and J. B. Norman. 2007. Using GIS to generate spatially balanced random survey designs for natural resource applications. Environmental Management 40:134-146.

United States Geological Survey. 2011. (DRAFT) DOI Southeast Climate Science Center Operational and Science Plan. U.S. Geological Survey Open-File Report. 2011-0000 (publication pending).

Visser, M. E., and C. Both. 2005. Shifts in phenology due to global climate change: The need for a yardstick. Proceedings of the Royal Society 272:2561-2569.

Watson, C., and K. Malloy. 2006. The South Atlantic migratory bird initiative implementation plan: An integrated approach to conservation of all birds across all habitats, version 3.1. Atlantic Coast Joint Venture. Available online: http://www.acjv.org/documents/SAMBI_Plan3.2.pdf.

Whittaker, R. H. 1972. Evolution and measurement of species diversity. Taxon 21:213-251.

Wolda, H. 1983. Diversity, diversity indices and tropical cockroaches. Oecologia 58:290–298.

Wright, C. J., E. Thompson, B. A. Blankley, M. W. Byrne, T. Curtis, and M. B. Gregory. 2011. Summary of weather and climate monitoring in Southeast Coast Network parks, 2010. Natural Resource Data Series NPS/SECN/NRDS—2011/XXX. National Park Service, Fort Collins, Colorado.

Appendix A. Birds known to occur at FOSU

Table A-1. Birds known to occur at Fort Sumter National Monument based upon records in NPSpecies (2011) and those detected during this sampling effort.

Order	Family	Scientific Name	Common Name	NPSpecies	VCP 2010
Anseriformes	Anatidae	*Aythya affinis*	Lesser Scaup	X	
Anseriformes	Anatidae	*Bucephala albeola*	Bufflehead	X	
Anseriformes	Anatidae	*Lophodytes cucullatus*	Hooded Merganser	X	
Anseriformes	Anatidae	*Melanitta perspicillata*	Surf Scoter	X	
Anseriformes	Anatidae	*Mergus serrator*	Red-breasted Merganser	X	
Gaviiformes	Gaviidae	*Gavia immer*	Common Loon	X	
Gaviiformes	Gaviidae	*Gavia stellata*	Red-throated Loon	X	
Podicipediformes	Podicipedidae	*Podiceps auritus*	Horned Grebe	X	
Podicipediformes	Podicipedidae	*Podilymbus podiceps*	Pied-billed Grebe	X	
Suliformes	Sulidae	*Morus bassanus*	Northern Gannet	X	
Suliformes	Phalacrocoracidae	*Phalacrocorax auritus*	Double-crested Cormorant	X	X
Pelecaniformes	Pelecanidae	*Pelecanus occidentalis*	Brown Pelican	X	X
Pelecaniformes	Ardeidae	*Ardea alba*	Great Egret	X	
Pelecaniformes	Ardeidae	*Ardea herodias*	Great Blue Heron	X	
Pelecaniformes	Ardeidae	*Butorides virescens*	Green Heron		X
Pelecaniformes	Ardeidae	*Egretta thula*	Snowy Egret	X	
Pelecaniformes	Ardeidae	*Egretta tricolor*	Tricolored Heron	X	
Pelecaniformes	Threskiornithidae	*Eudocimus albus*	White Ibis	X	
Accipitriformes	Cathartidae	*Cathartes aura*	Turkey Vulture	X	
Accipitriformes	Cathartidae	*Coragyps atratus*	Black Vulture	X	
Accipitriformes	Pandionidae	*Pandion haliaetus*	Osprey	X	X
Accipitriformes	Accipitridae	*Accipiter cooperii*	Cooper's Hawk	X	
Accipitriformes	Accipitridae	*Accipiter striatus*	Sharp-shinned Hawk	X	
Accipitriformes	Accipitridae	*Aquila chrysaetos*	Golden Eagle	X	
Accipitriformes	Accipitridae	*Buteo lineatus*	Red-shouldered Hawk	X	
Accipitriformes	Accipitridae	*Circus cyaneus*	Northern Harrier	X	
Accipitriformes	Accipitridae	*Haliaeetus leucocephalus*	Bald Eagle	X	
Falconiformes	Falconidae	*Falco columbarius*	Merlin	X	
Falconiformes	Falconidae	*Falco peregrinus*	Peregrine Falcon	X	
Falconiformes	Falconidae	*Falco sparverius*	American Kestrel	X	
Gruiformes	Rallidae	*Porzana carolina*	Sora	X	
Gruiformes	Rallidae	*Rallus elegans*	King Rail	X	
Charadriiformes	Charadriidae	*Charadrius melodus*	Piping Plover	X	
Charadriiformes	Charadriidae	*Charadrius semipalmatus*	Semipalmated Plover	X	
Charadriiformes	Charadriidae	*Charadrius vociferus*	Killdeer	X	
Charadriiformes	Charadriidae	*Pluvialis squatarola*	Black-bellied Plover	X	
Charadriiformes	Haematopodidae	*Haematopus palliatus*	American Oystercatcher	X	
Charadriiformes	Recurvirostridae	*Himantopus mexicanus*	Black-necked Stilt	X	
Charadriiformes	Scolopacidae	*Arenaria interpres*	Ruddy Turnstone	X	
Charadriiformes	Scolopacidae	*Calidris alba*	Sanderling	X	
Charadriiformes	Scolopacidae	*Calidris alpina*	Dunlin	X	
Charadriiformes	Scolopacidae	*Calidris canutus*	Red Knot	X	

Table A-1. Continued.

Order	Family	Scientific Name	Common Name	NPSpecies	VCP 2010
Charadriiformes	Scolopacidae	*Calidris fuscicollis*	White-rumped Sandpiper	X	
Charadriiformes	Scolopacidae	*Calidris maritima*	Purple Sandpiper	X	
Charadriiformes	Scolopacidae	*Calidris mauri*	Western Sandpiper	X	
Charadriiformes	Scolopacidae	*Calidris minutilla*	Least Sandpiper	X	
Charadriiformes	Scolopacidae	*Calidris pusilla*	Semipalmated Sandpiper	X	X
Charadriiformes	Scolopacidae	*Catoptrophorus semipalmatus*	Willet	X	
Charadriiformes	Scolopacidae	*Gallinago delicata*	Wilson's Snipe	X	
Charadriiformes	Scolopacidae	*Limnodromus griseus*	Short-billed Dowitcher	X	
Charadriiformes	Scolopacidae	*Numenius phaeopus*	Whimbrel	X	
Charadriiformes	Scolopacidae	*Tringa flavipes*	Lesser Yellowlegs	X	
Charadriiformes	Scolopacidae	*Tringa melanoleuca*	Greater Yellowlegs	X	
Charadriiformes	Laridae	*Larus argentatus*	Herring Gull	X	
Charadriiformes	Laridae	*Larus atricilla*	Laughing Gull	X	X
Charadriiformes	Laridae	*Larus delawarensis*	Ring-billed Gull	X	
Charadriiformes	Laridae	*Larus fuscus*	Lesser Black-backed Gull	X	
Charadriiformes	Laridae	*Larus marinus*	Great Black-backed Gull	X	
Charadriiformes	Laridae	*Larus philadelphia*	Bonaparte's Gull	X	
Charadriiformes	Laridae	*Rynchops niger*	Black Skimmer	X	
Charadriiformes	Laridae	*Sterna antillarum*	Least Tern	X	X
Charadriiformes	Laridae	*Sterna forsteri*	Forster's Tern	X	
Charadriiformes	Laridae	*Sterna hirundo*	Common Tern	X	
Charadriiformes	Laridae	*Sterna maxima*	Royal Tern	X	X
Charadriiformes	Laridae	*Sterna sandvicensis*	Sandwich Tern	X	
Columbiformes	Columbidae	*Columba livia*	Rock Pigeon	X	
Columbiformes	Columbidae	*Columbina passerina*	Common Ground-Dove	X	
Columbiformes	Columbidae	*Streptopelia decaocto*	Eurasian Collared-Dove	X	X
Columbiformes	Columbidae	*Zenaida asiatica*	White-winged Dove	X	
Columbiformes	Columbidae	*Zenaida macroura*	Mourning Dove	X	X
Cuculiformes	Cuculidae	*Coccyzus americanus*	Yellow-billed Cuckoo	X	
Cuculiformes	Cuculidae	*Coccyzus erythropthalmus*	Black-billed Cuckoo	X	
Strigiformes	Strigidae	*Bubo virginianus*	Great Horned Owl	X	
Strigiformes	Strigidae	*Megascops asio*	Eastern Screech-Owl	X	
Caprimulgiformes	Caprimulgidae	*Caprimulgus carolinensis*	Chuck-will's-widow	X	
Caprimulgiformes	Caprimulgidae	*Caprimulgus vociferus*	Eastern Whip-poor-will	X	
Caprimulgiformes	Caprimulgidae	*Chordeiles minor*	Common Nighthawk	X	
Apodiformes	Apodidae	*Chaetura pelagica*	Chimney Swift		X
Apodiformes	Trochilidae	*Archilochus colubris*	Ruby-throated Hummingbird	X	
Piciformes	Picidae	*Melanerpes carolinus*	Red-bellied Woodpecker	X	
Piciformes	Picidae	*Melanerpes erythrocephalus*	Red-headed Woodpecker	X	
Piciformes	Picidae	*Picoides pubescens*	Downy Woodpecker	X	
Piciformes	Picidae	*Picoides villosus*	Hairy Woodpecker	X	
Piciformes	Picidae	*Sphyrapicus varius*	Yellow-bellied Sapsucker	X	

Table A-1. Continued.

Order	Family	Scientific Name	Common Name	NPSpecies	VCP 2010
Passeriformes	Tyrannidae	*Empidonax alnorum*	Alder Flycatcher	X	
Passeriformes	Tyrannidae	*Empidonax flaviventris*	Yellow-bellied Flycatcher	X	
Passeriformes	Tyrannidae	*Empidonax minimus*	Least Flycatcher	X	
Passeriformes	Tyrannidae	*Empidonax traillii*	Willow Flycatcher	X	
Passeriformes	Tyrannidae	*Sayornis phoebe*	Eastern Phoebe	X	
Passeriformes	Tyrannidae	*Tyrannus dominicensis*	Gray Kingbird	X	
Passeriformes	Tyrannidae	*Tyrannus tyrannus*	Eastern Kingbird		X
Passeriformes	Laniidae	*Lanius ludovicianus*	Loggerhead Shrike	X	
Passeriformes	Vireonidae	*Vireo griseus*	White-eyed Vireo	X	X
Passeriformes	Vireonidae	*Vireo olivaceus*	Red-eyed Vireo	X	X
Passeriformes	Vireonidae	*Vireo solitarius*	Blue-headed Vireo	X	
Passeriformes	Corvidae	*Corvus brachyrhynchos*	American Crow	X	
Passeriformes	Corvidae	*Corvus ossifragus*	Fish Crow	X	X
Passeriformes	Corvidae	*Cyanocitta cristata*	Blue Jay		X
Passeriformes	Alaudidae	*Eremophila alpestris*	Horned Lark	X	
Passeriformes	Hirundinidae	*Hirundo rustica*	Barn Swallow	X	X
Passeriformes	Hirundinidae	*Progne subis*	Purple Martin	X	
Passeriformes	Hirundinidae	*Riparia riparia*	Bank Swallow	X	
Passeriformes	Hirundinidae	*Stelgidopteryx serripennis*	Northern Rough-winged Swallow	X	
Passeriformes	Hirundinidae	*Tachycineta bicolor*	Tree Swallow	X	
Passeriformes	Paridae	*Baeolophus bicolor*	Tufted Titmouse	X	
Passeriformes	Paridae	*Poecile carolinensis*	Carolina Chickadee	X	X
Passeriformes	Sittidae	*Sitta canadensis*	Red-breasted Nuthatch	X	
Passeriformes	Sittidae	*Sitta carolinensis*	White-breasted Nuthatch	X	
Passeriformes	Certhiidae	*Certhia americana*	Brown Creeper	X	
Passeriformes	Troglodytidae	*Cistothorus palustris*	Marsh Wren	X	
Passeriformes	Troglodytidae	*Cistothorus platensis*	Sedge Wren	X	
Passeriformes	Troglodytidae	*Thryothorus ludovicianus*	Carolina Wren	X	X
Passeriformes	Troglodytidae	*Troglodytes aedon*	House Wren	X	X
Passeriformes	Troglodytidae	*Troglodytes troglodytes*	Winter Wren	X	
Passeriformes	Regulidae	*Regulus calendula*	Ruby-crowned Kinglet	X	
Passeriformes	Turdidae	*Catharus fuscescens*	Veery	X	
Passeriformes	Turdidae	*Catharus ustulatus*	Swainson's Thrush	X	
Passeriformes	Turdidae	*Sialia sialis*	Eastern Bluebird	X	X
Passeriformes	Turdidae	*Turdus migratorius*	American Robin	X	X
Passeriformes	Mimidae	*Dumetella carolinensis*	Gray Catbird	X	X
Passeriformes	Mimidae	*Mimus polyglottos*	Northern Mockingbird	X	X
Passeriformes	Mimidae	*Toxostoma rufum*	Brown Thrasher	X	
Passeriformes	Sturnidae	*Sturnus vulgaris*	European Starling	X	X
Passeriformes	Motacillidae	*Anthus rubescens*	American Pipit	X	
Passeriformes	Bombycillidae	*Bombycilla cedrorum*	Cedar Waxwing	X	
Passeriformes	Calcariidae	*Plectrophenax nivalis*	Snow Bunting	X	

Table A-1. Continued.

Order	Family	Scientific Name	Common Name	NPSpecies	VCP 2010
Passeriformes	Parulidae	*Dendroica caerulescens*	Black-throated Blue Warbler	X	
Passeriformes	Parulidae	*Dendroica coronata*	Yellow-rumped Warbler	X	
Passeriformes	Parulidae	*Dendroica discolor*	Prairie Warbler	X	
Passeriformes	Parulidae	*Dendroica dominica*	Yellow-throated Warbler	X	
Passeriformes	Parulidae	*Dendroica magnolia*	Magnolia Warbler	X	
Passeriformes	Parulidae	*Dendroica palmarum*	Palm Warbler	X	
Passeriformes	Parulidae	*Dendroica petechia*	Yellow Warbler	X	
Passeriformes	Parulidae	*Dendroica pinus*	Pine Warbler	X	
Passeriformes	Parulidae	*Dendroica striata*	Blackpoll Warbler	X	
Passeriformes	Parulidae	*Dendroica tigrina*	Cape May Warbler	X	
Passeriformes	Parulidae	*Geothlypis trichas*	Common Yellowthroat	X	
Passeriformes	Parulidae	*Helmitheros vermivorus*	Worm-eating Warbler	X	
Passeriformes	Parulidae	*Icteria virens*	Yellow-breasted Chat	X	
Passeriformes	Parulidae	*Limnothlypis swainsonii*	Swainson's Warbler	X	
Passeriformes	Parulidae	*Mniotilta varia*	Black-and-white Warbler	X	
Passeriformes	Parulidae	*Oporornis agilis*	Connecticut Warbler	X	
Passeriformes	Parulidae	*Oporornis formosus*	Kentucky Warbler	X	
Passeriformes	Parulidae	*Oporornis philadelphia*	Mourning Warbler	X	
Passeriformes	Parulidae	*Parula americana*	Northern Parula	X	
Passeriformes	Parulidae	*Protonotaria citrea*	Prothonotary Warbler	X	X
Passeriformes	Parulidae	*Seiurus aurocapillus*	Ovenbird	X	
Passeriformes	Parulidae	*Seiurus noveboracensis*	Northern Waterthrush	X	
Passeriformes	Parulidae	*Setophaga ruticilla*	American Redstart	X	
Passeriformes	Parulidae	*Vermivora celata*	Orange-crowned Warbler	X	
Passeriformes	Parulidae	*Vermivora peregrina*	Tennessee Warbler	X	
Passeriformes	Parulidae	*Vermivora ruficapilla*	Nashville Warbler	X	
Passeriformes	Parulidae	*Wilsonia citrina*	Hooded Warbler	X	
Passeriformes	Parulidae	*Wilsonia pusilla*	Wilson's Warbler	X	
Passeriformes	Emberizidae	*Ammodramus maritimus*	Seaside Sparrow		X
Passeriformes	Emberizidae	*Junco hyemalis*	Dark-eyed Junco	X	
Passeriformes	Emberizidae	*Melospiza georgiana*	Swamp Sparrow	X	X
Passeriformes	Emberizidae	*Melospiza lincolnii*	Lincoln's Sparrow	X	
Passeriformes	Emberizidae	*Melospiza melodia*	Song Sparrow	X	
Passeriformes	Emberizidae	*Passerculus sandwichensis*	Savannah Sparrow	X	
Passeriformes	Emberizidae	*Passerella iliaca*	Fox Sparrow	X	
Passeriformes	Emberizidae	*Pipilo erythrophthalmus*	Eastern Towhee	X	
Passeriformes	Emberizidae	*Pooecetes gramineus*	Vesper Sparrow	X	
Passeriformes	Emberizidae	*Spizella passerina*	Chipping Sparrow	X	
Passeriformes	Emberizidae	*Spizella pusilla*	Field Sparrow	X	
Passeriformes	Emberizidae	*Zonotrichia albicollis*	White-throated Sparrow	X	X
Passeriformes	Emberizidae	*Zonotrichia leucophrys*	White-crowned Sparrow	X	
Passeriformes	Cardinalidae	*Cardinalis cardinalis*	Northern Cardinal	X	X

Table A-1. Continued.

Order	Family	Scientific Name	Common Name	NPSpecies	VCP 2010
Passeriformes	Cardinalidae	*Guiraca caerulea*	Blue Grosbeak	X	
Passeriformes	Cardinalidae	*Passerina ciris*	Painted Bunting	X	X
Passeriformes	Cardinalidae	*Passerina cyanea*	Indigo Bunting	X	
Passeriformes	Cardinalidae	*Piranga olivacea*	Scarlet Tanager	X	
Passeriformes	Icteridae	*Agelaius phoeniceus*	Red-winged Blackbird	X	
Passeriformes	Icteridae	*Euphagus carolinus*	Rusty Blackbird	X	
Passeriformes	Icteridae	*Molothrus ater*	Brown-headed Cowbird	X	
Passeriformes	Icteridae	*Molothrus bonariensis*	Shiny Cowbird	X	
Passeriformes	Icteridae	*Quiscalus major*	Boat-tailed Grackle	X	X
Passeriformes	Icteridae	*Quiscalus quiscula*	Common Grackle	X	X
Passeriformes	Icteridae	*Sturnella magna*	Eastern Meadowlark	X	
Passeriformes	Icteridae	*Xanthocephalus xanthocephalus*	Yellow-headed Blackbird	X	
Passeriformes	Fringillidae	*Carduelis tristis*	American Goldfinch	X	X
Passeriformes	Fringillidae	*Carpodacus mexicanus*	House Finch	X	X
Passeriformes	Passeridae	*Passer domesticus*	House Sparrow	X	X

Appendix B. Map of sampling locations with point labels.

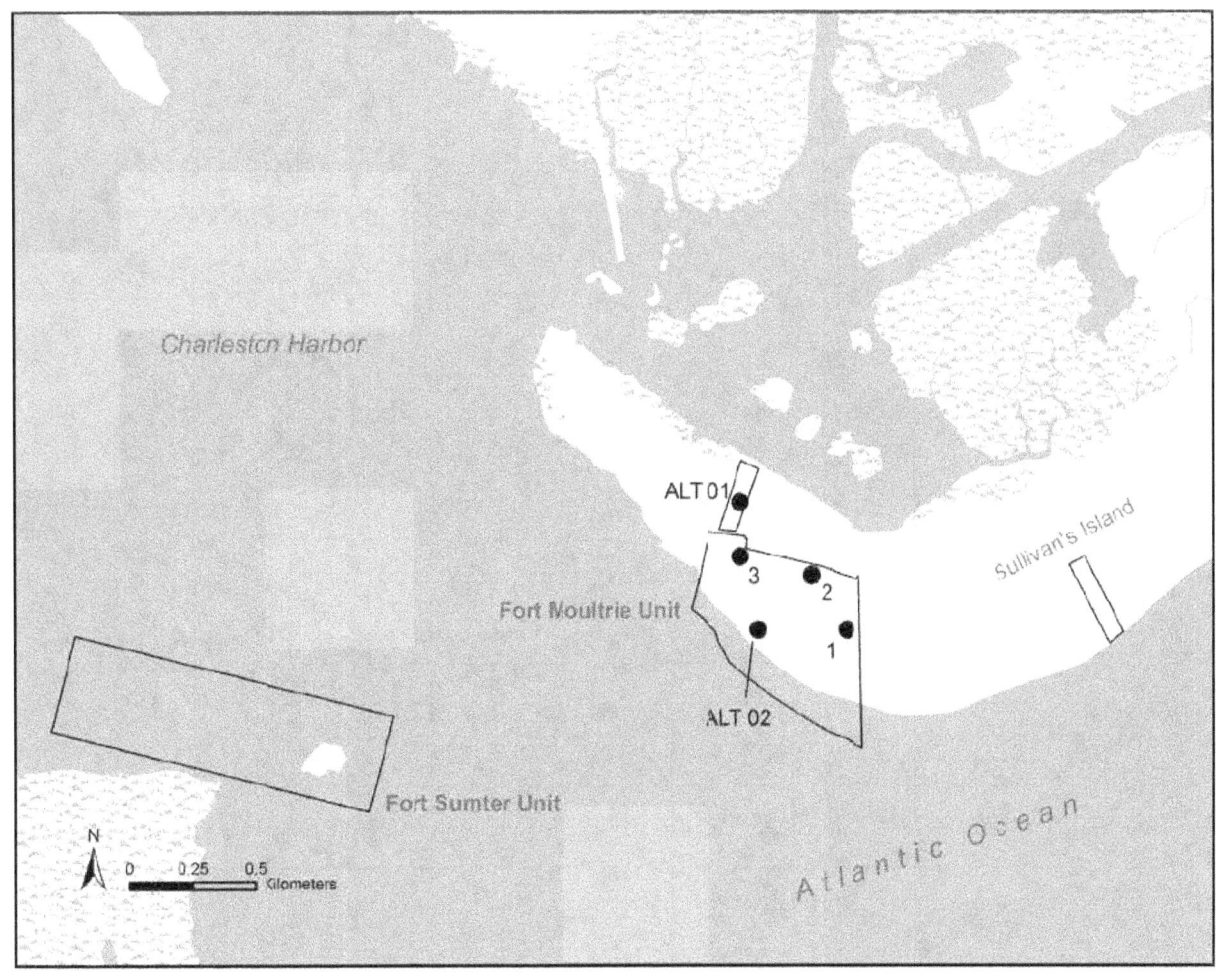

Figure B-1. Spatially-balanced random sampling locations at FOSU with labels, 2010.

Appendix C. Species detections by sampling location.

Table C-1. Species detected at each sampling location at FOSU, 2010. Refer to Appendix B for labeled sampling-locations.

Common Name	Sampling Location				
	1	2	3	A1	A2
Double-crested Cormorant					X
Brown Pelican		X	X	X	X
Green Heron				X	
Osprey				X	
Semipalmated Sandpiper					X
Laughing Gull	X		X		X
Least Tern				X	X
Royal Tern	X	X	X		X
Eurasian Collared-Dove	X	X	X	X	X
Mourning Dove	X	X	X	X	X
Chimney Swift	X	X	X	X	
Eastern Kingbird					X
White-eyed Vireo	X				
Red-eyed Vireo	X				
Blue Jay	X	X	X	X	X
Fish Crow	X			X	
Barn Swallow	X	X	X	X	X
Carolina Chickadee		X		X	
Carolina Wren	X		X		X
House Wren	X				X
Eastern Bluebird			X		
American Robin			X		
Gray Catbird					X
Northern Mockingbird	X	X	X	X	X
European Starling		X	X	X	
Prothonotary Warbler		X			
Seaside Sparrow				X	
Swamp Sparrow			X		
White-throated Sparrow	X		X		
Northern Cardinal	X	X	X	X	X
Painted Bunting					X
Common Grackle					X
Boat-tailed Grackle	X	X	X	X	X
House Finch	X	X		X	X
American Goldfinch	X		X		X
House Sparrow	X	X	X		

Appendix D. Distribution Maps

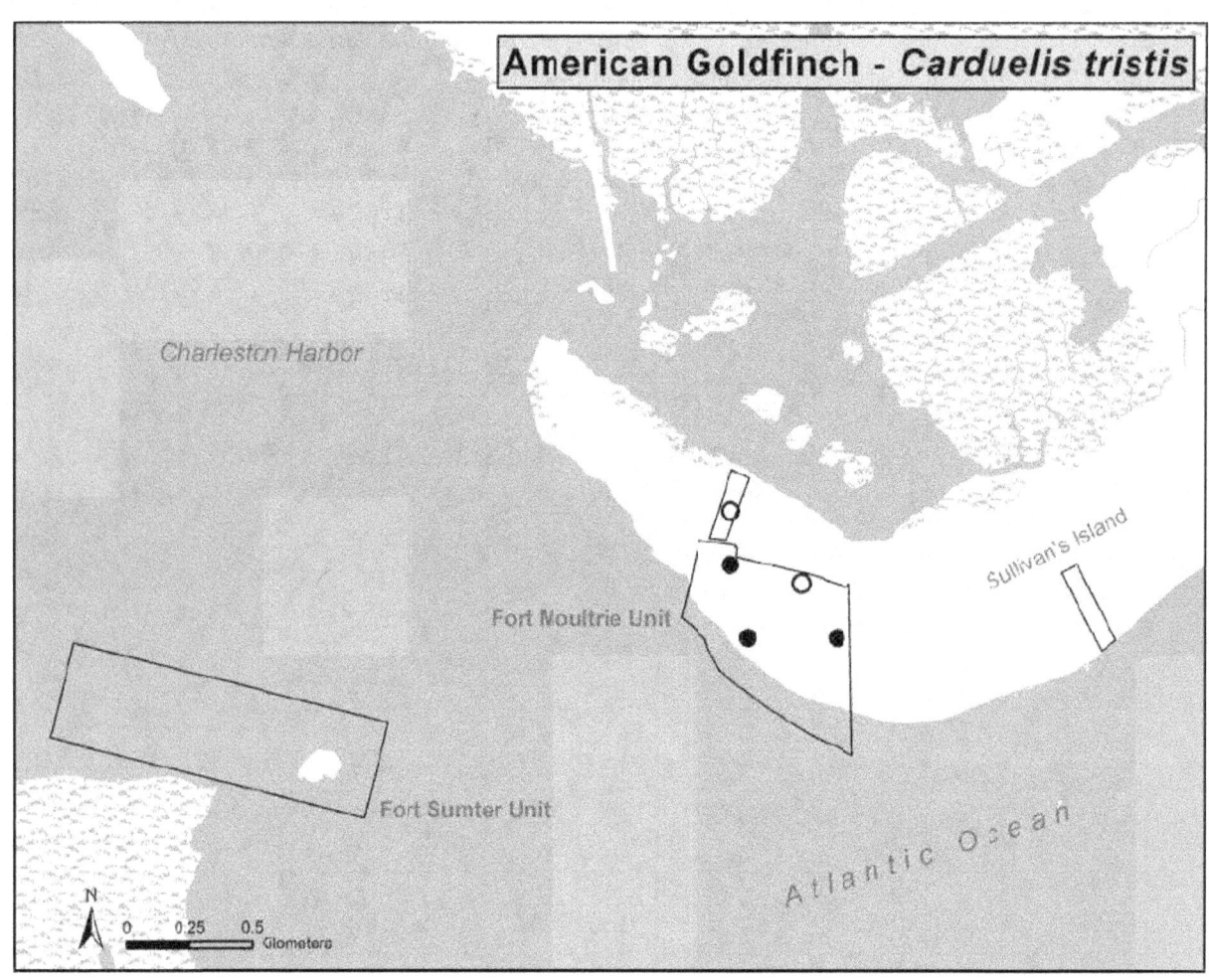

Figure D-1. Sampling locations where American Goldfinch (*Carduelis tristis*) was detected at FOSU, 2010. ● = detected, ○ = not detected.

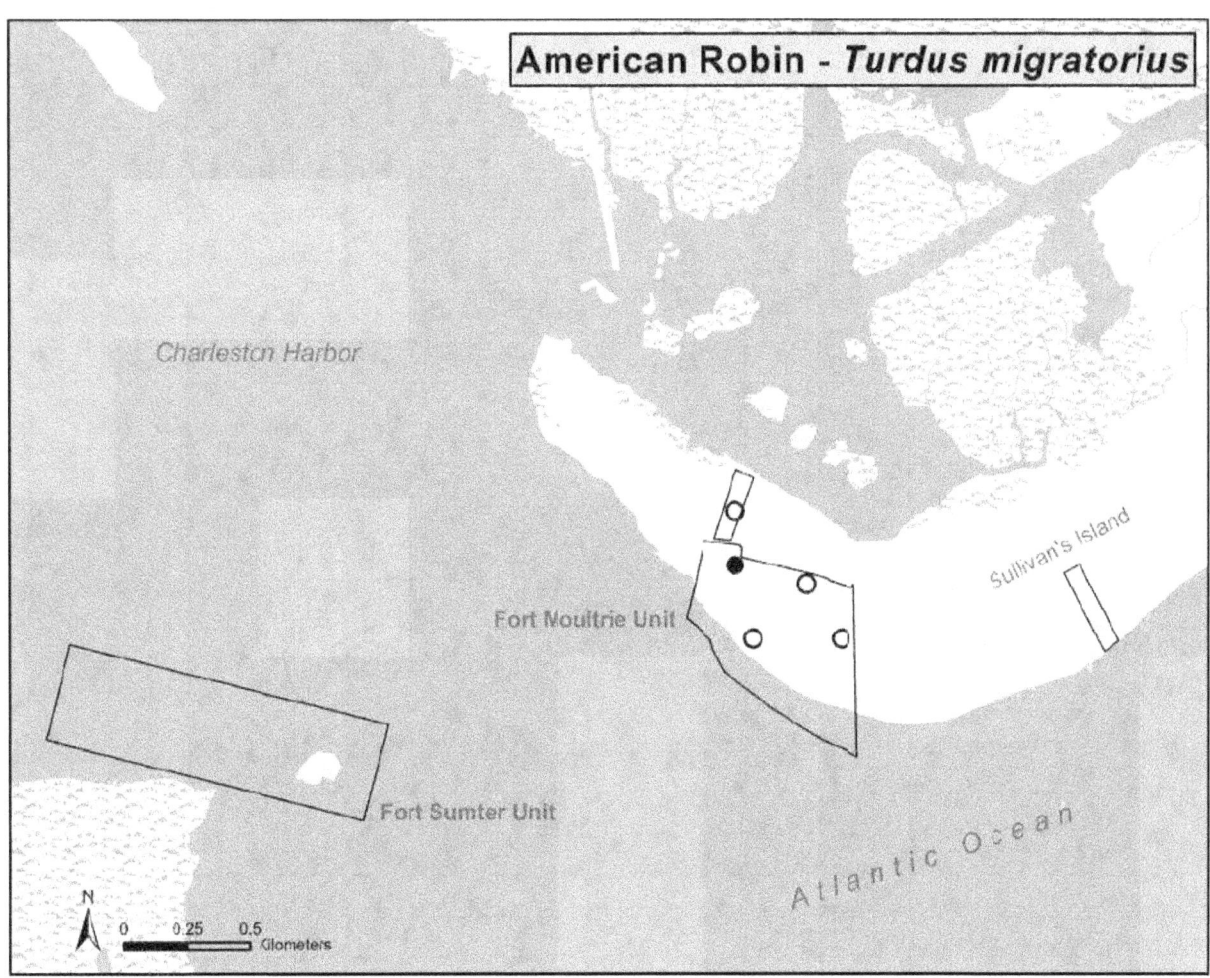

Figure D-2. Sampling locations where American Robin (*Turdus migratori is*) was detected at FOSU, 2010. ● = detected, ○ = not detected.

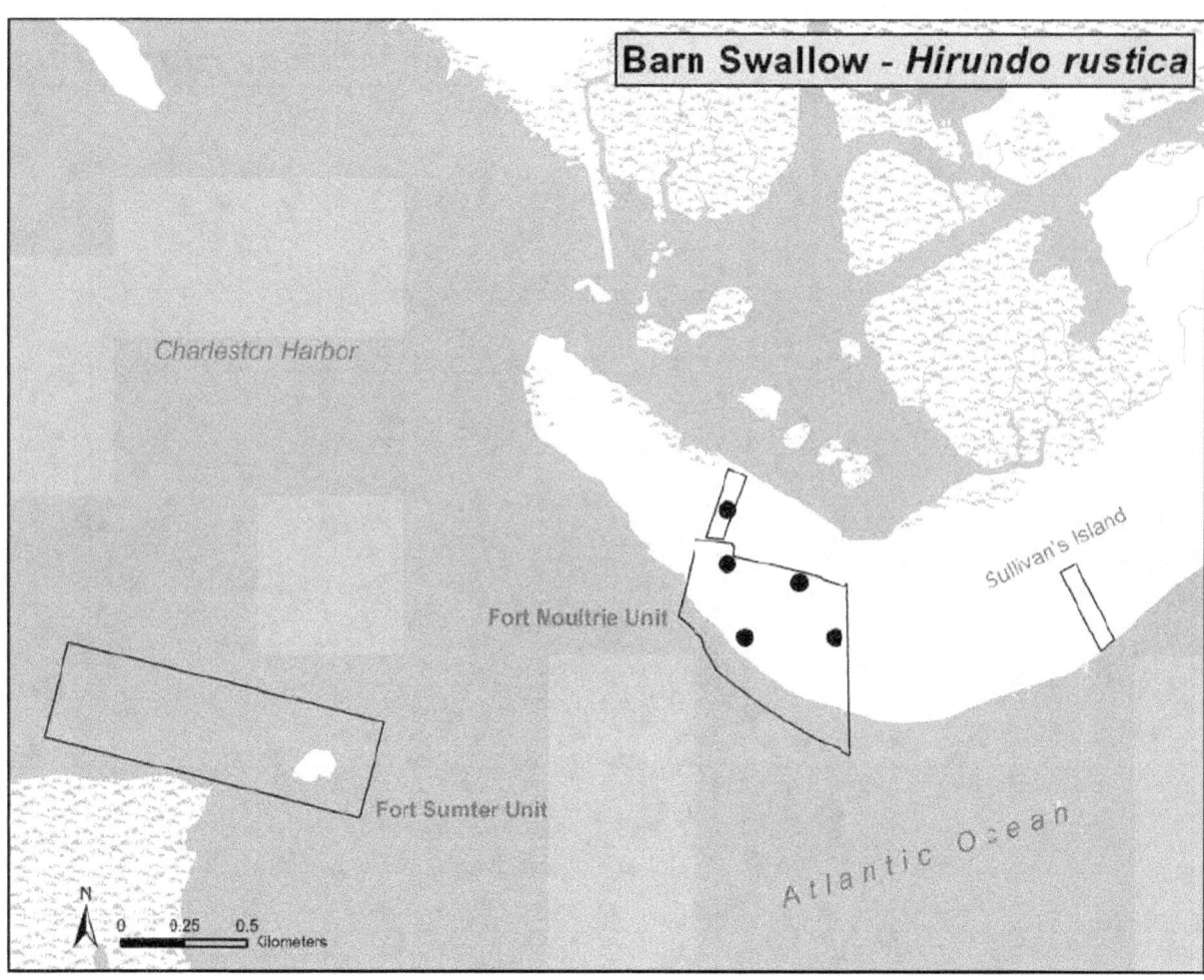

Figure D-3. Sampling locations where Barn Swallow (*Hirun 'o rustica*) was detected at FOSU, 2010. ● = detected, ○ = not dete∘ted.

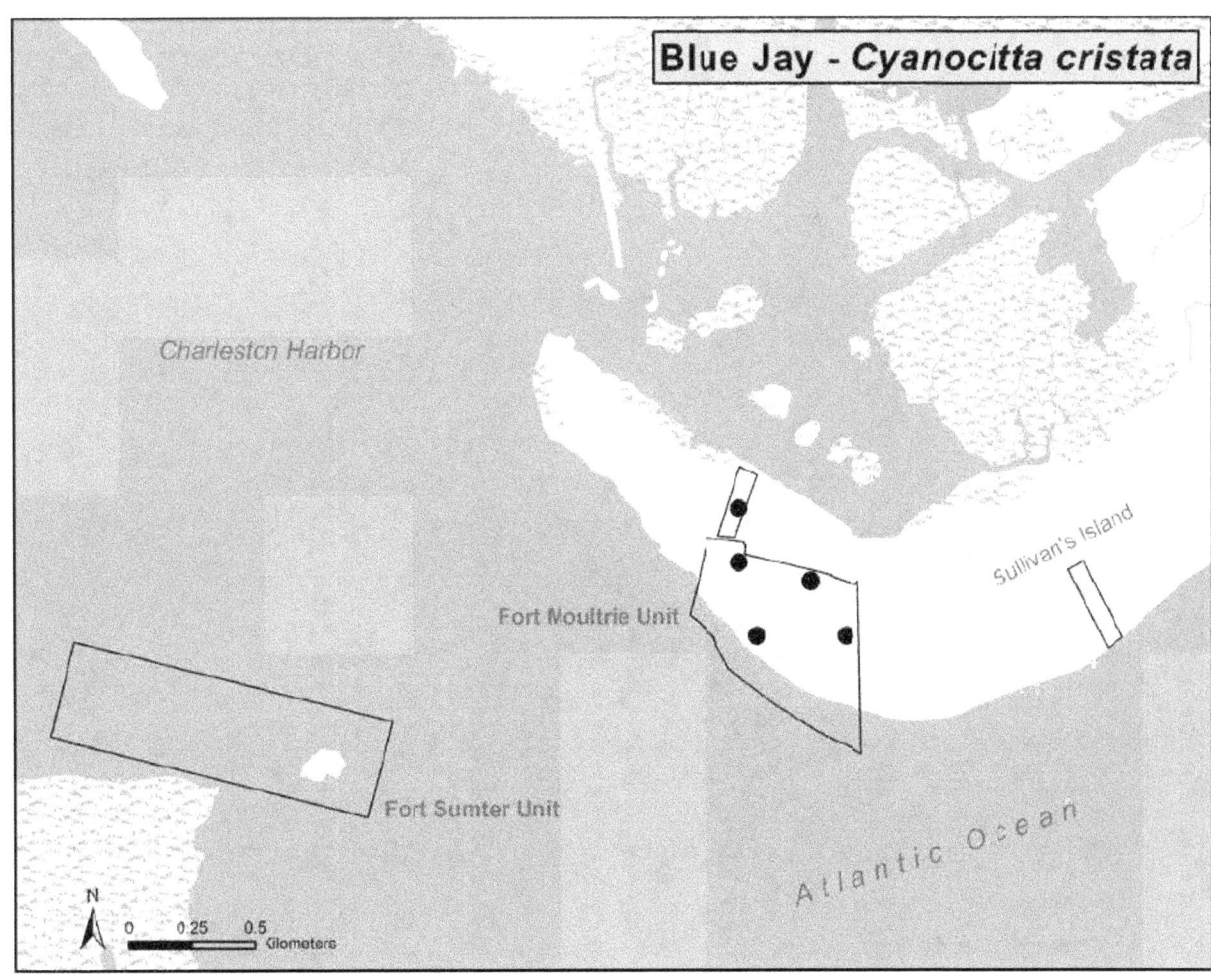

Figure D-4. Sampling locations where Blue Jay (*Cyanocitta cristata*) was detected at FOSU, 2010. ● = detected, ○ = not detected.

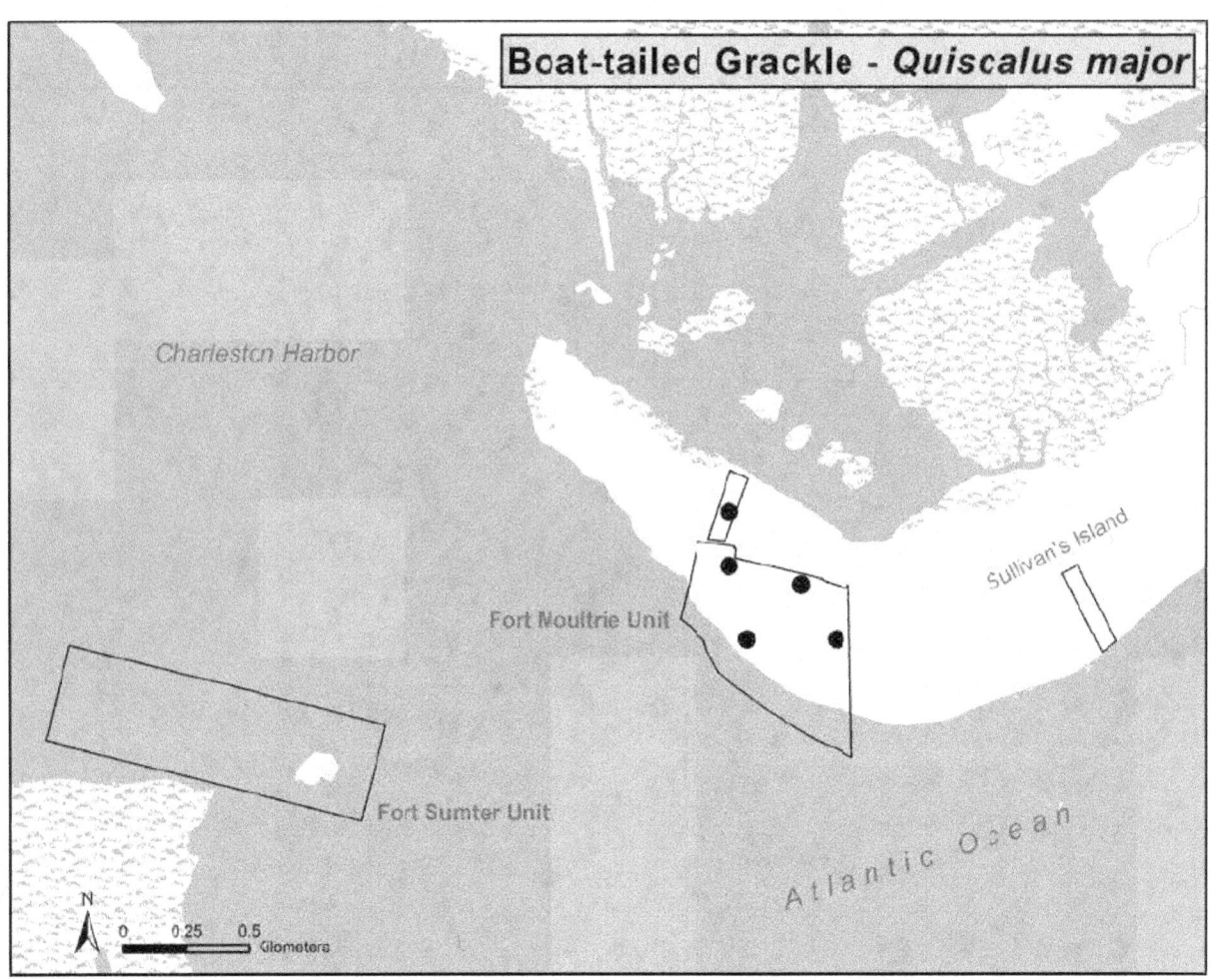

Figure D-5. Sampling locations where Boat-tailed Grackle (*Quiscalus major*) was detected at FOSU, 2010. ● = detected, ○ = not detected.

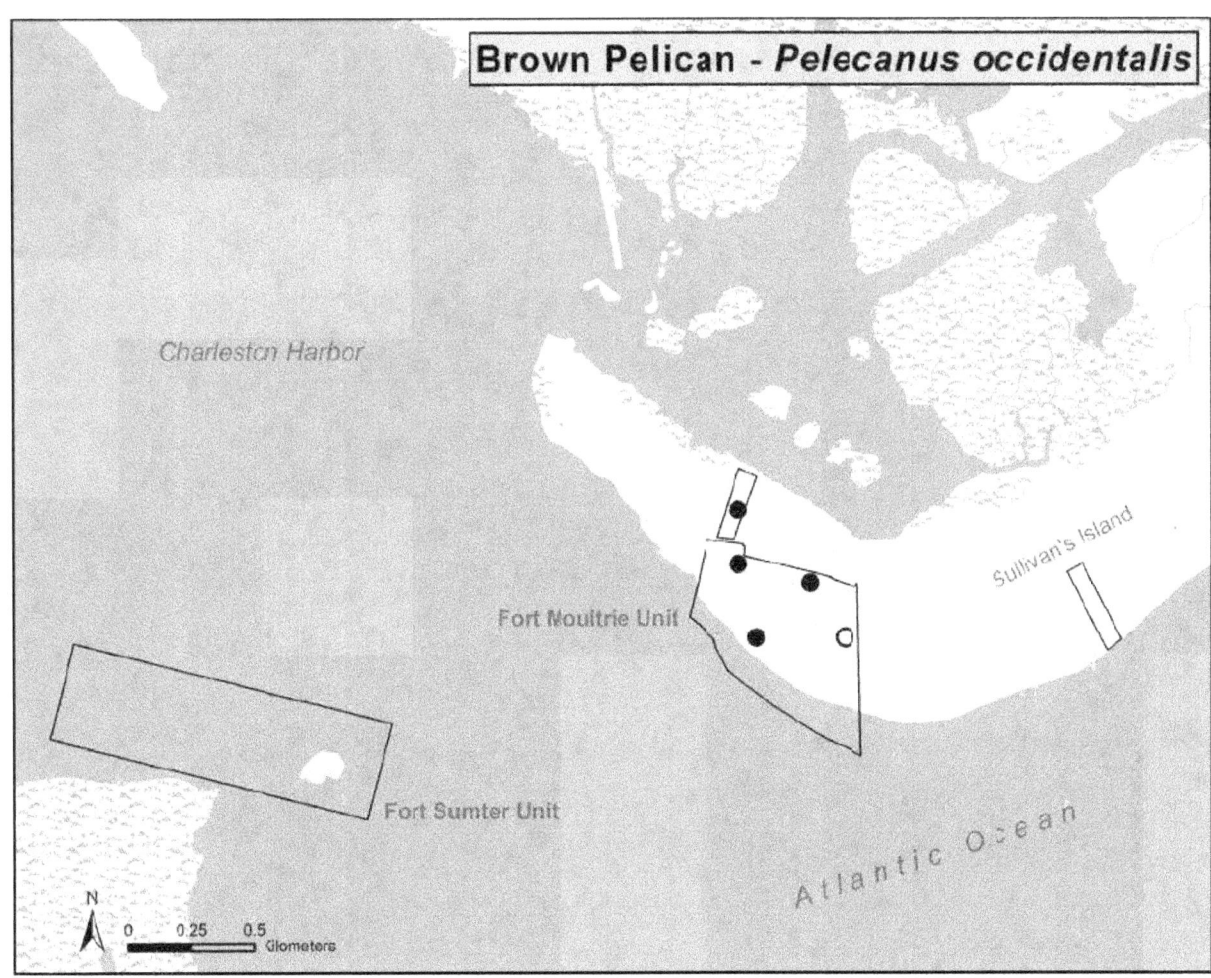

Figure D-6. Sampling locations where Brown Pelican (*Pelecanus occide·talis*) was detected at FOSU, 2010. ● = detected, ○ = not detected.

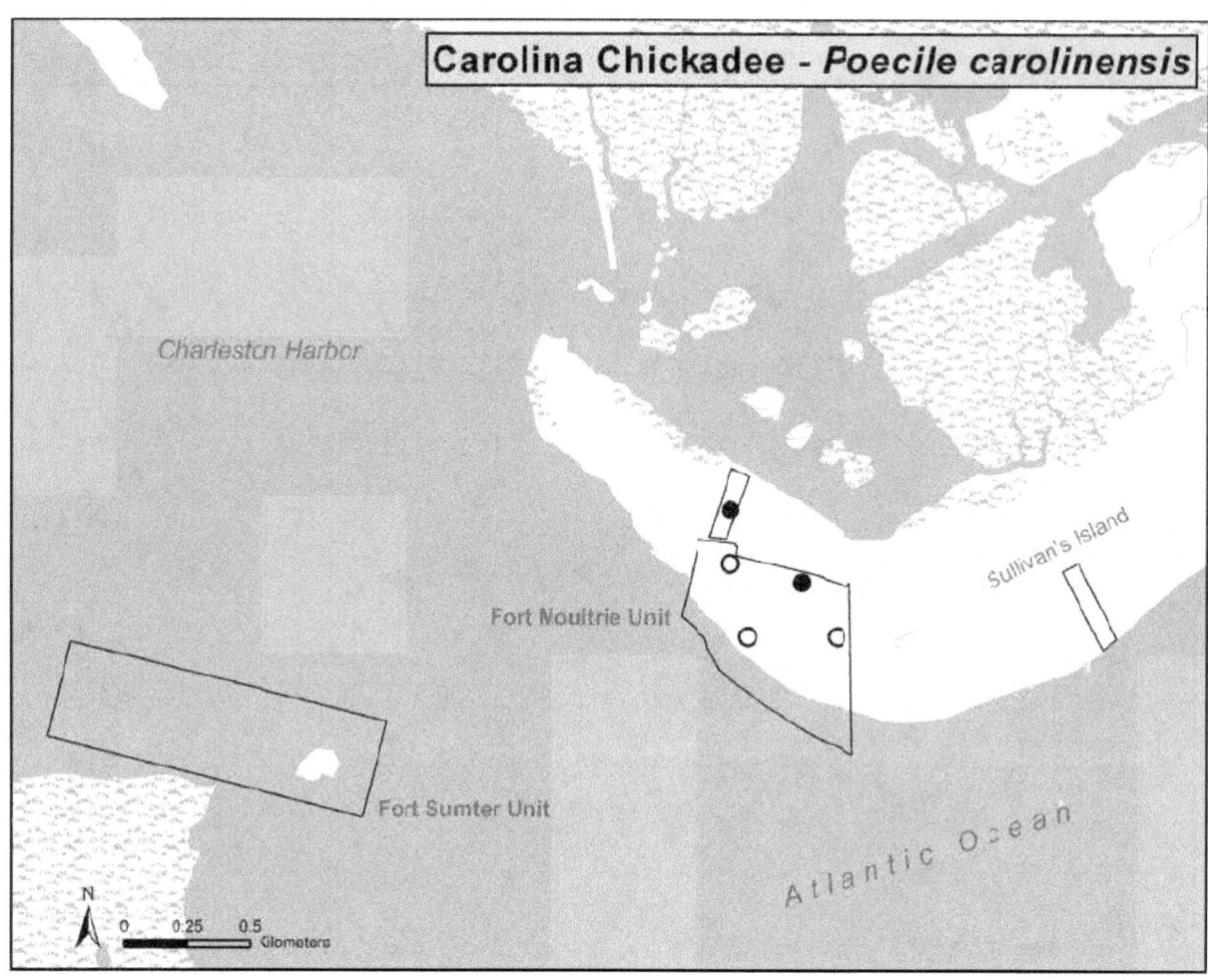

Figure D-7. Sampling locations where Carolina Chickadee (*Poecile carolinensis*) was detected at FOSU, 2010. ● = detected, ○ = not detected.

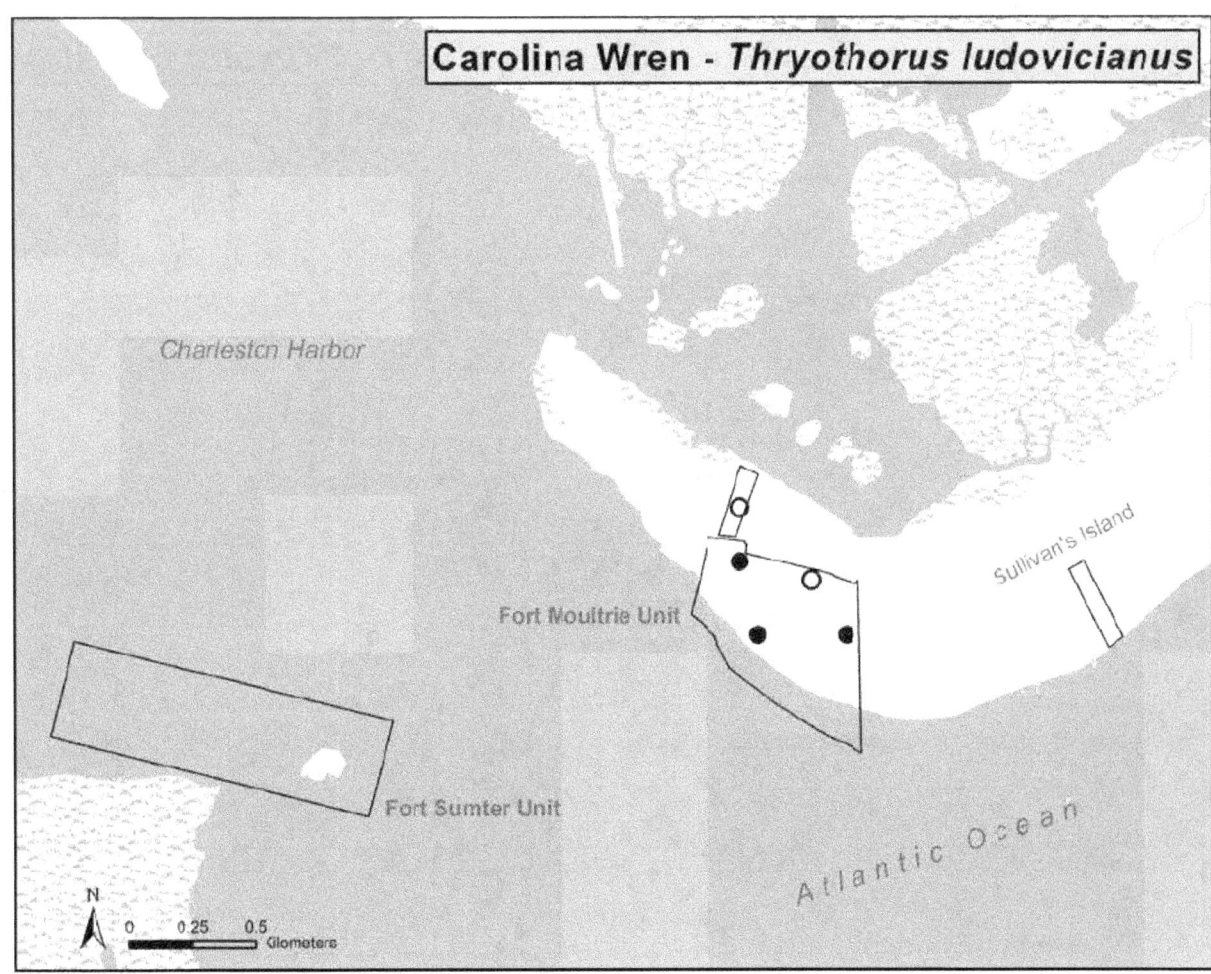

Figure D-8. Sampling locations where Carolina Wren (*Thryothorus ludovicianus*) was detected at FOSU, 2010. ● = detected, ○ = not detected.

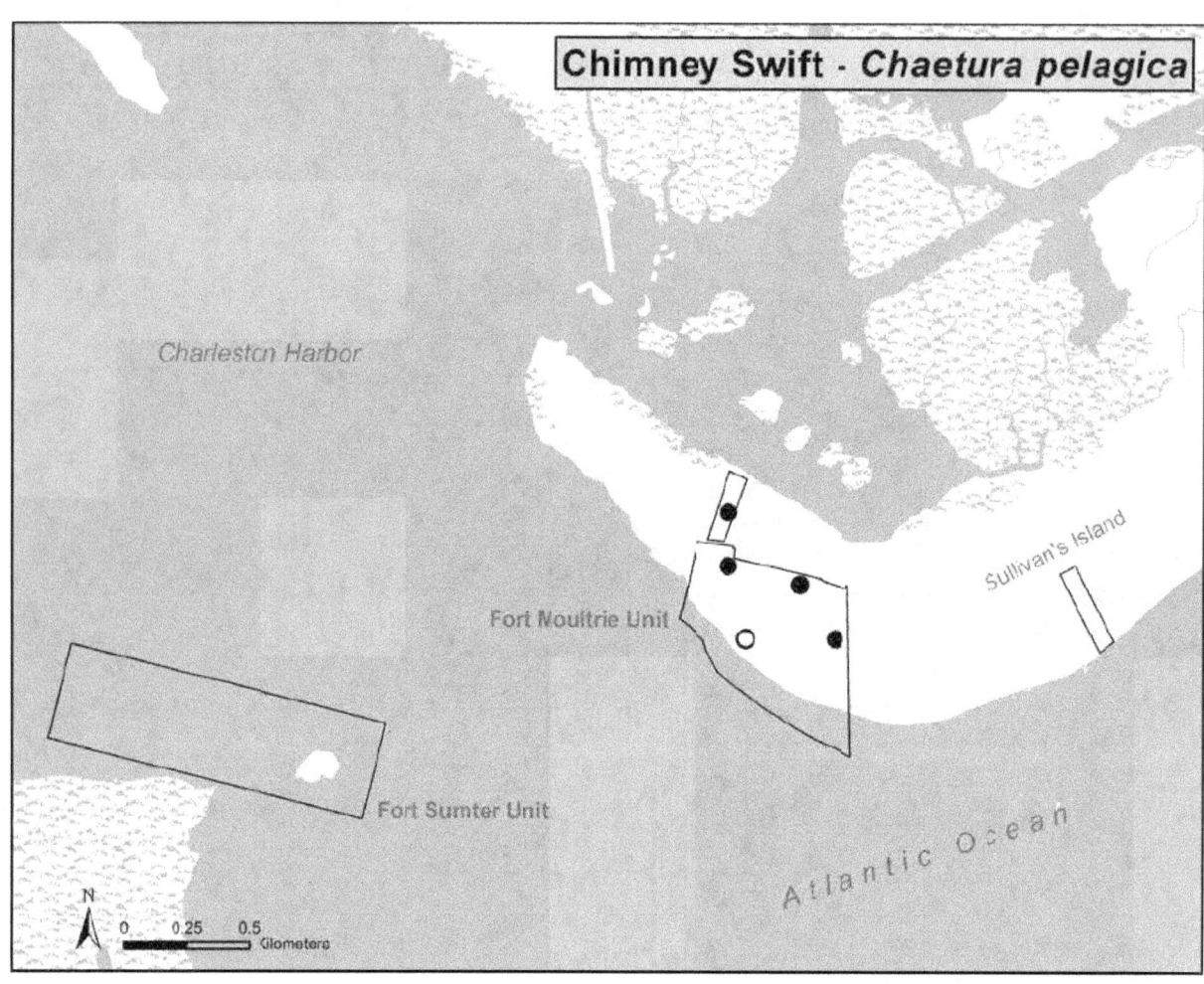

Figure D-9. Sampling locations where Chimney Swift (*Chae'ura pelagica*) was detected at FOSU, 2010.
● = detected, ○ = not letected.

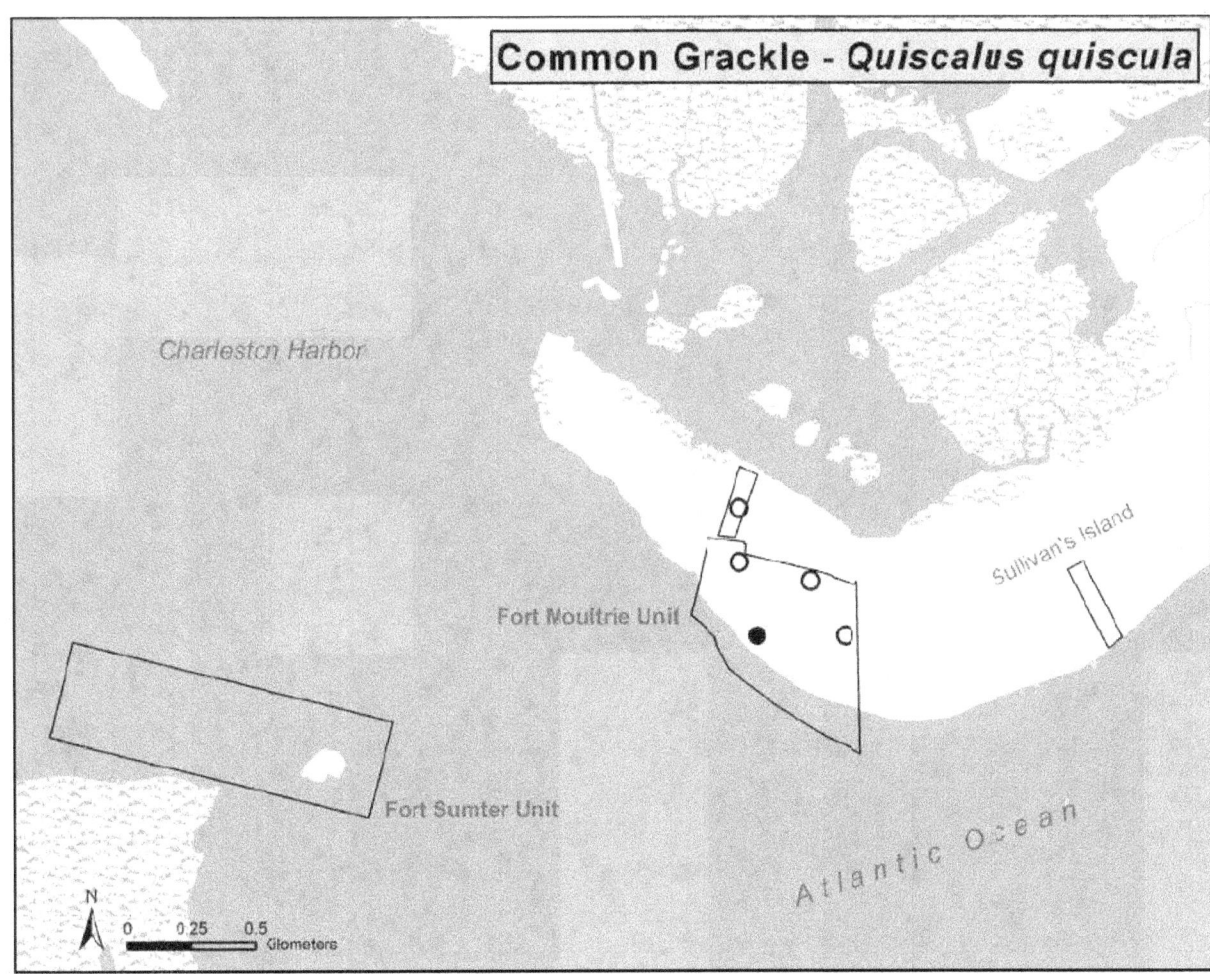

Figure D-10. Sampling locations where Common Grackle (*Quiscalus qui icula*) was detected at FOSU, 2010. ● = detected, ○ = not detected.

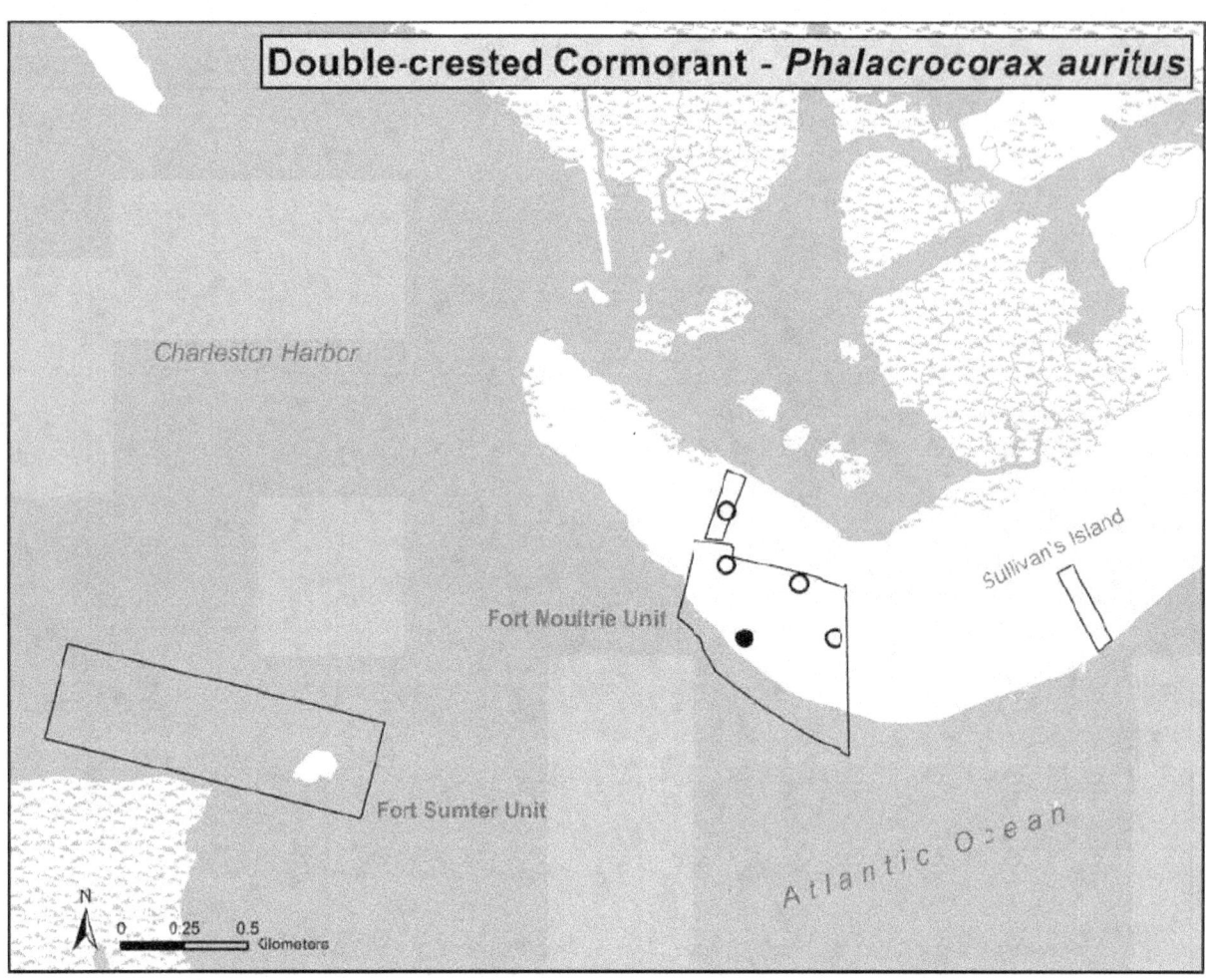

Figure D-11. Sampling locations where Double-crested Cormorant (*Phal icrocorax auritus*) was detected at FOSU, 2010. ● = d tected, ○ = not detected.

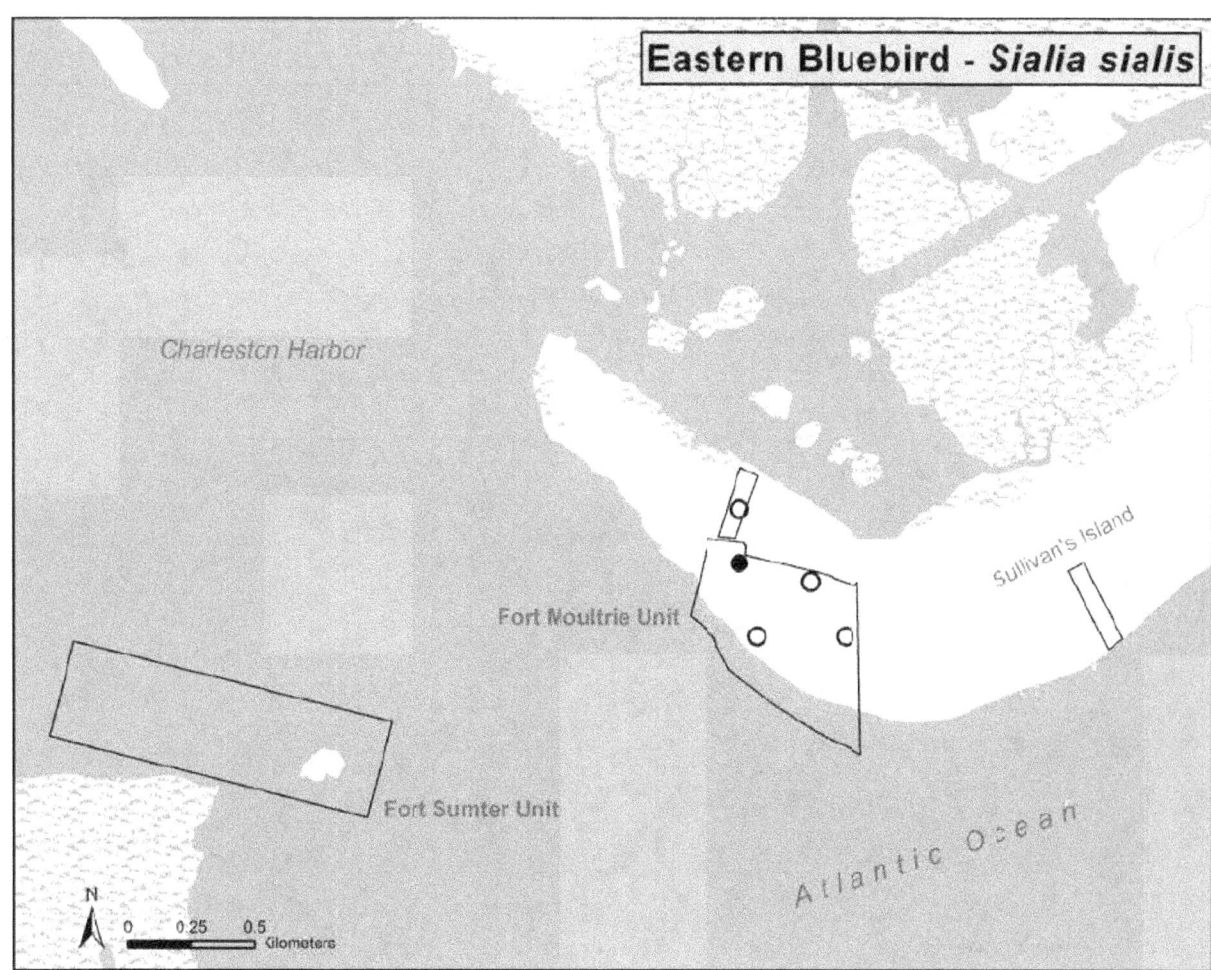

Figure D-12. Sampling locations where Eastern Bluebird (*Sialia sialis*) was detected at FOSU, 2010. ● = detected, ○ = not detected.

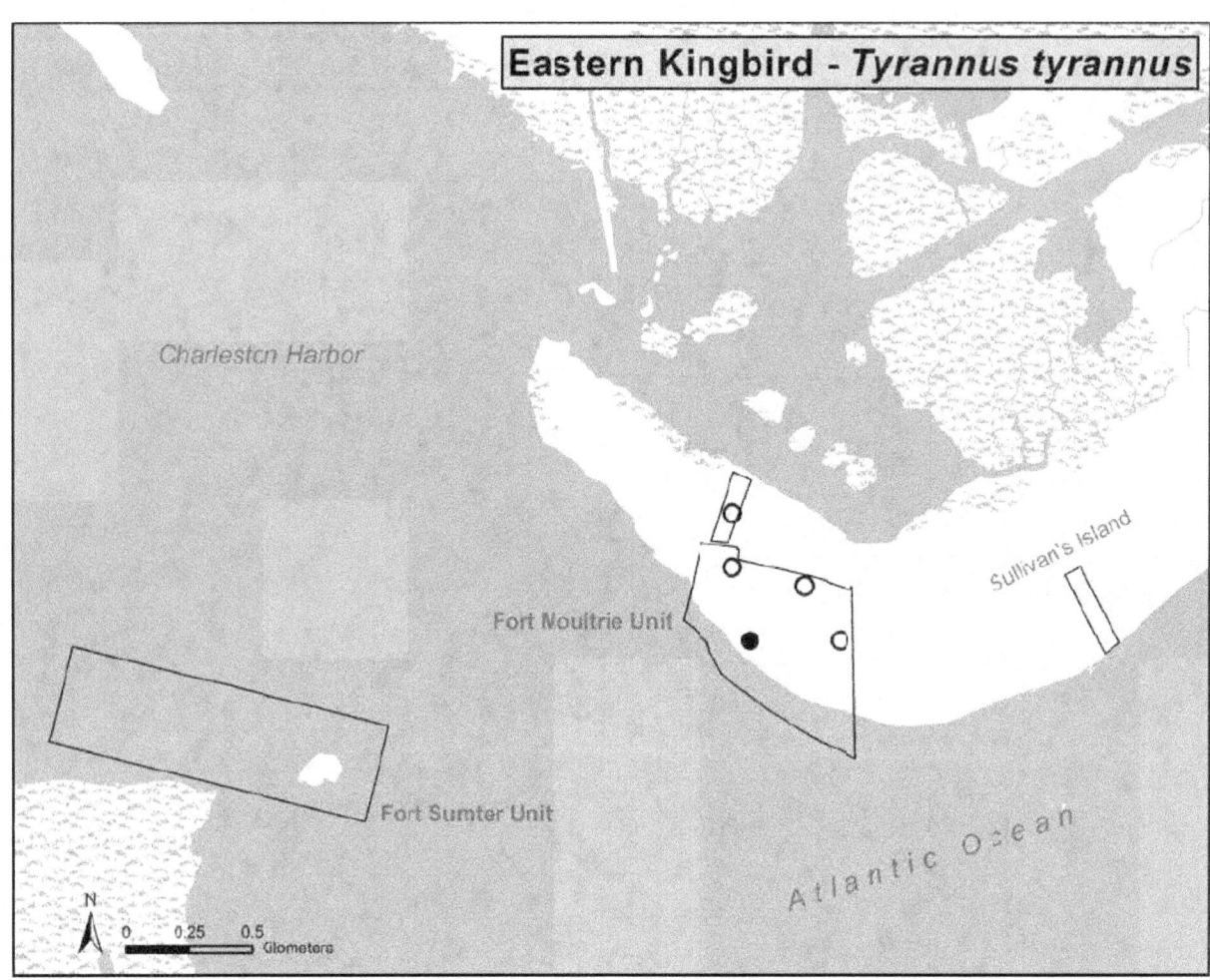

Figure D-13. Sampling locations where Eastern Kingbird (*T rannus tyrannus*) was detected at FOSU, 2010. ● = detected, ○ = not detected.

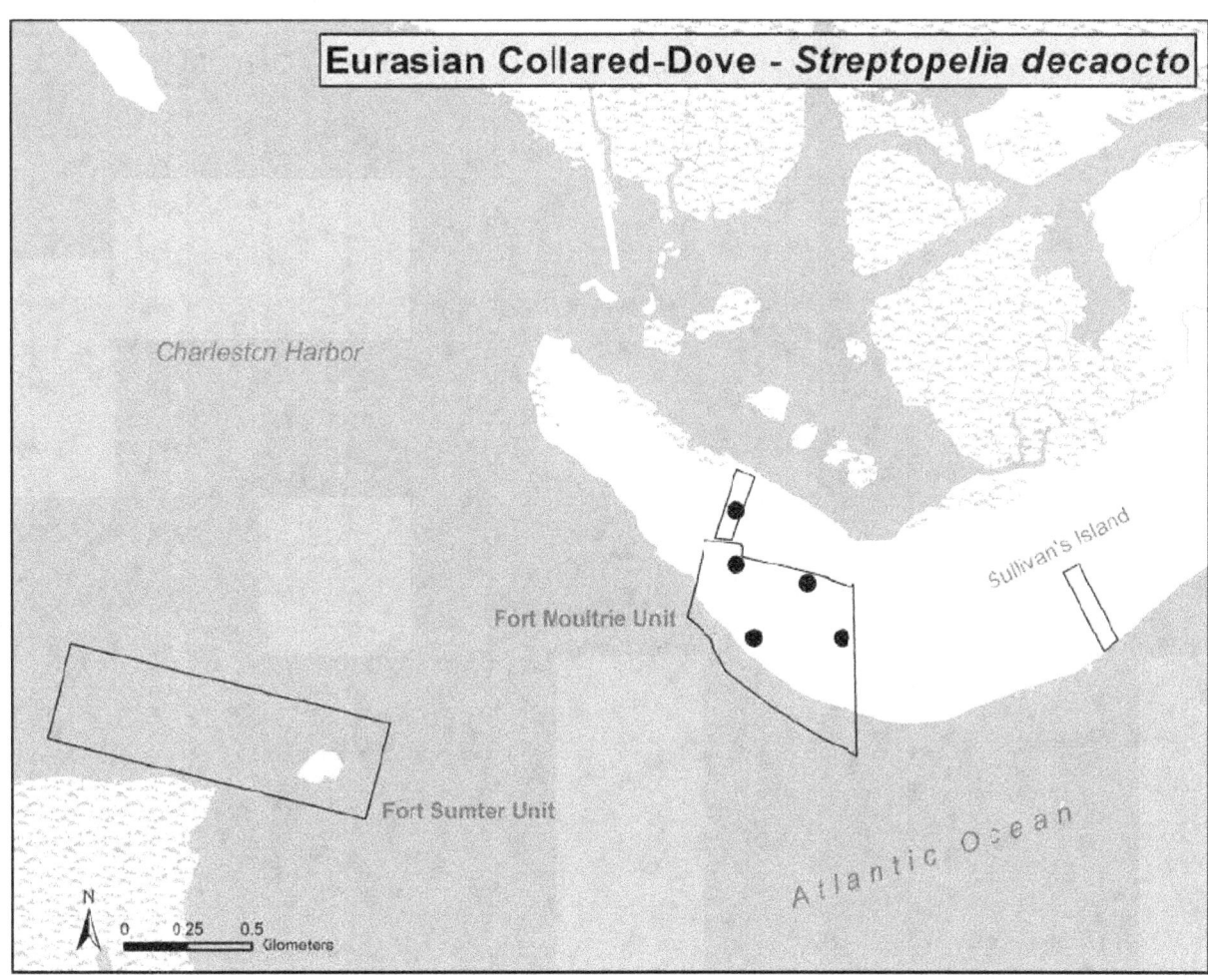

Figure D-14. Sampling locations where Eurasian Collared-Dove (*Strepto ᵓelia decaocto*) was detected at FOSU, 2)10. ● = detected, ○ = not detected.

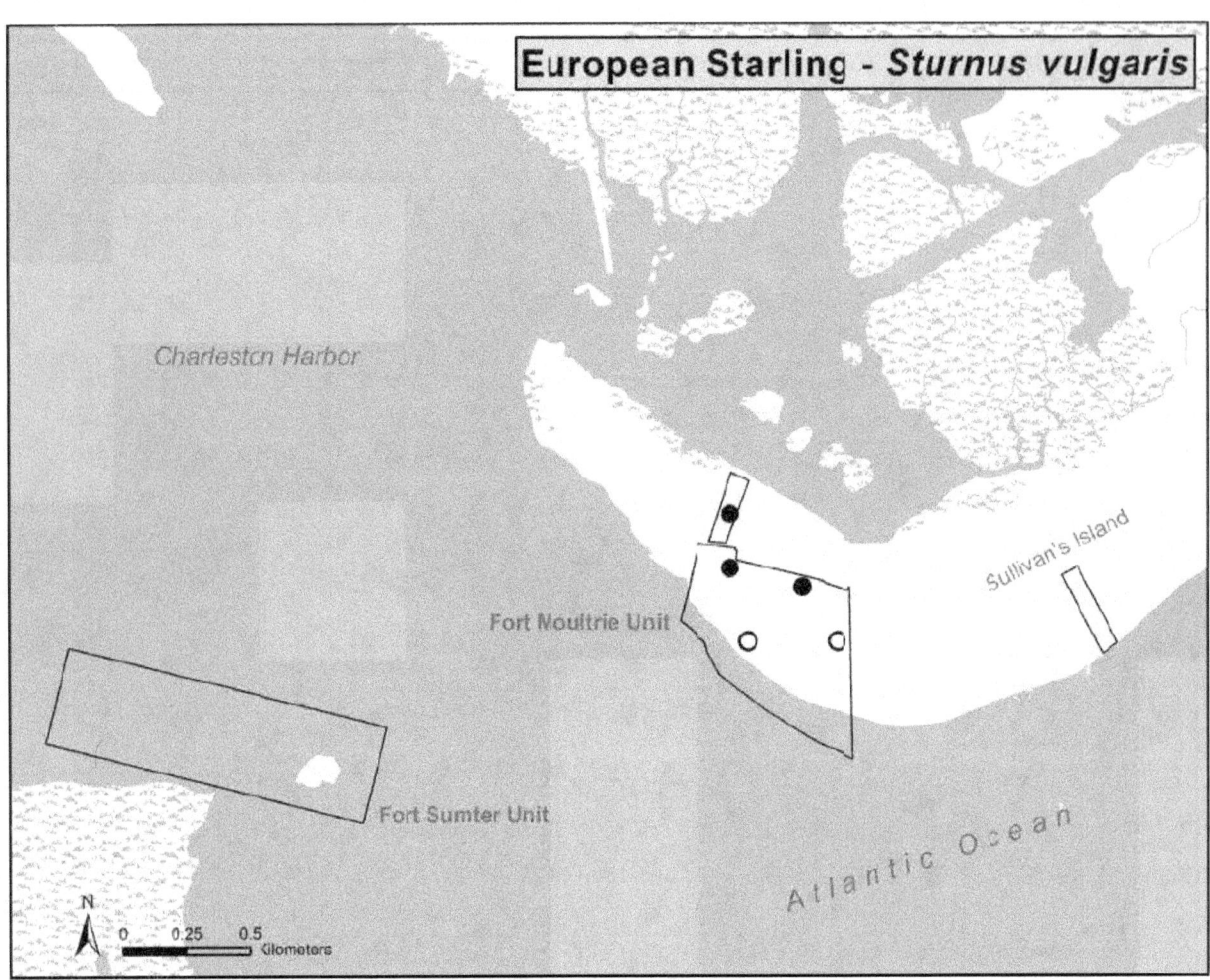

Figure D-15. Sampling locations where European Starling (*Sturnus vulgaris*) was detected at FOSU, 2010. ● = detected, ○ = not detected.

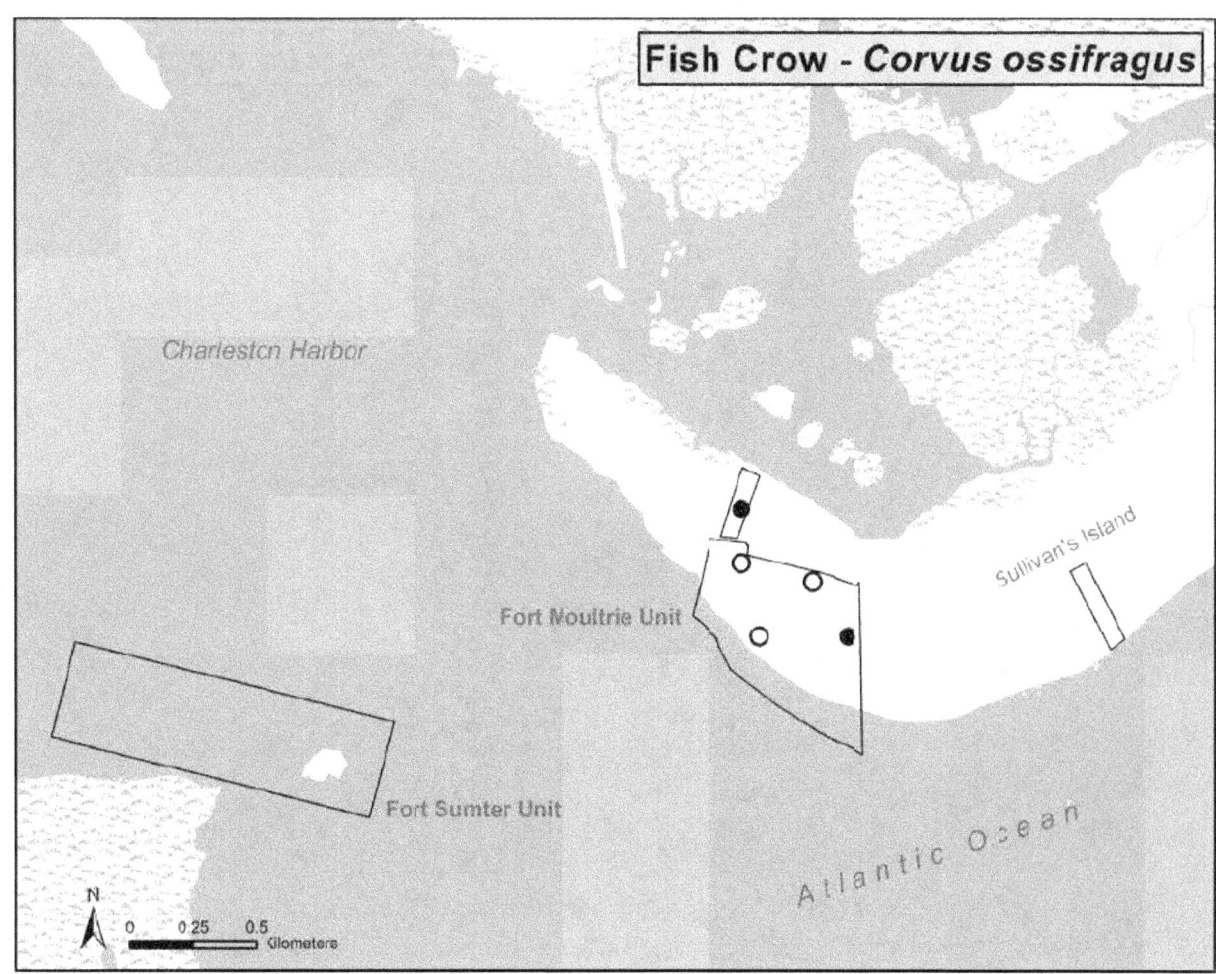

Figure D-16. Sampling locations where Fish Crow (*Corvus ossifragus*) was detected at FOSU, 2010. ● = detected, ○ = not detected.

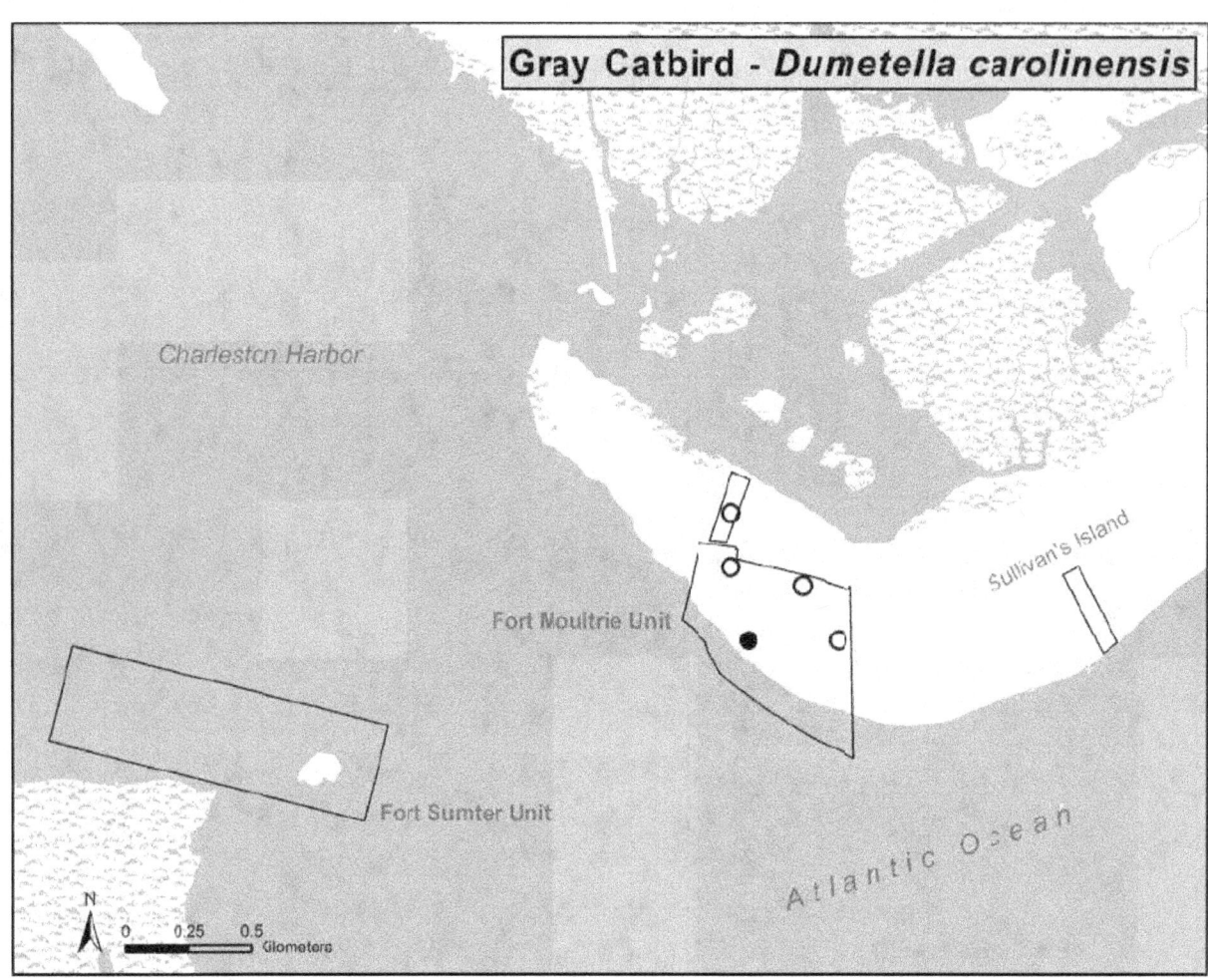

Figure D-17. Sampling locations where Gray Catbird (*Dumetella caroline nsis*) was detected at FOSU, 2010. ● = detected, ○ = not detected.

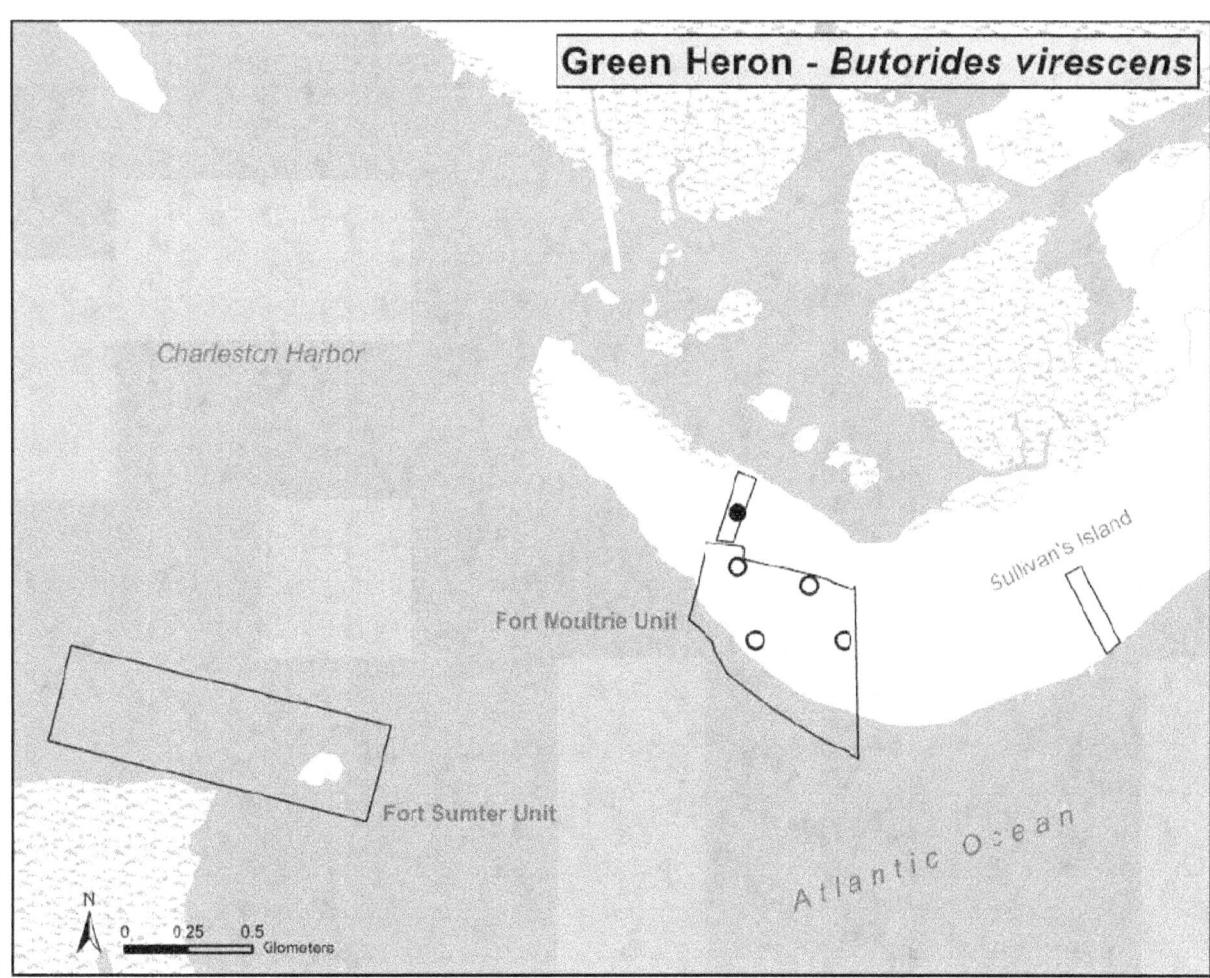

Figure D-18. Sampling locations where Green Heron (*Butorides virescens*) was detected at FOSU, 2010. ● = detected, ○ = not detected.

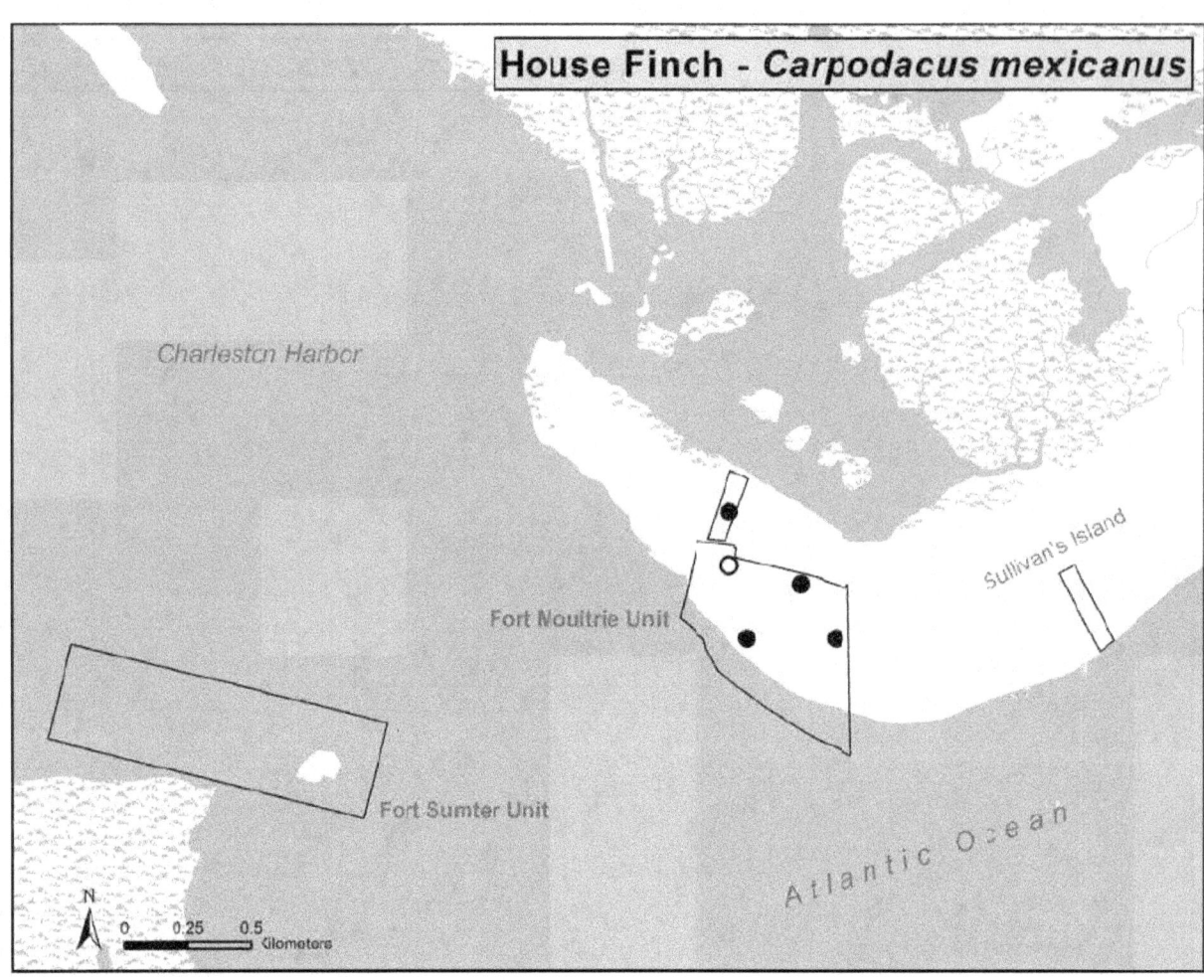

Figure D-19. Sampling locations where House Finch (*Carpodacus mexicanus*) was detected at FOSU, 2010. ● = detected, ○ = not detected.

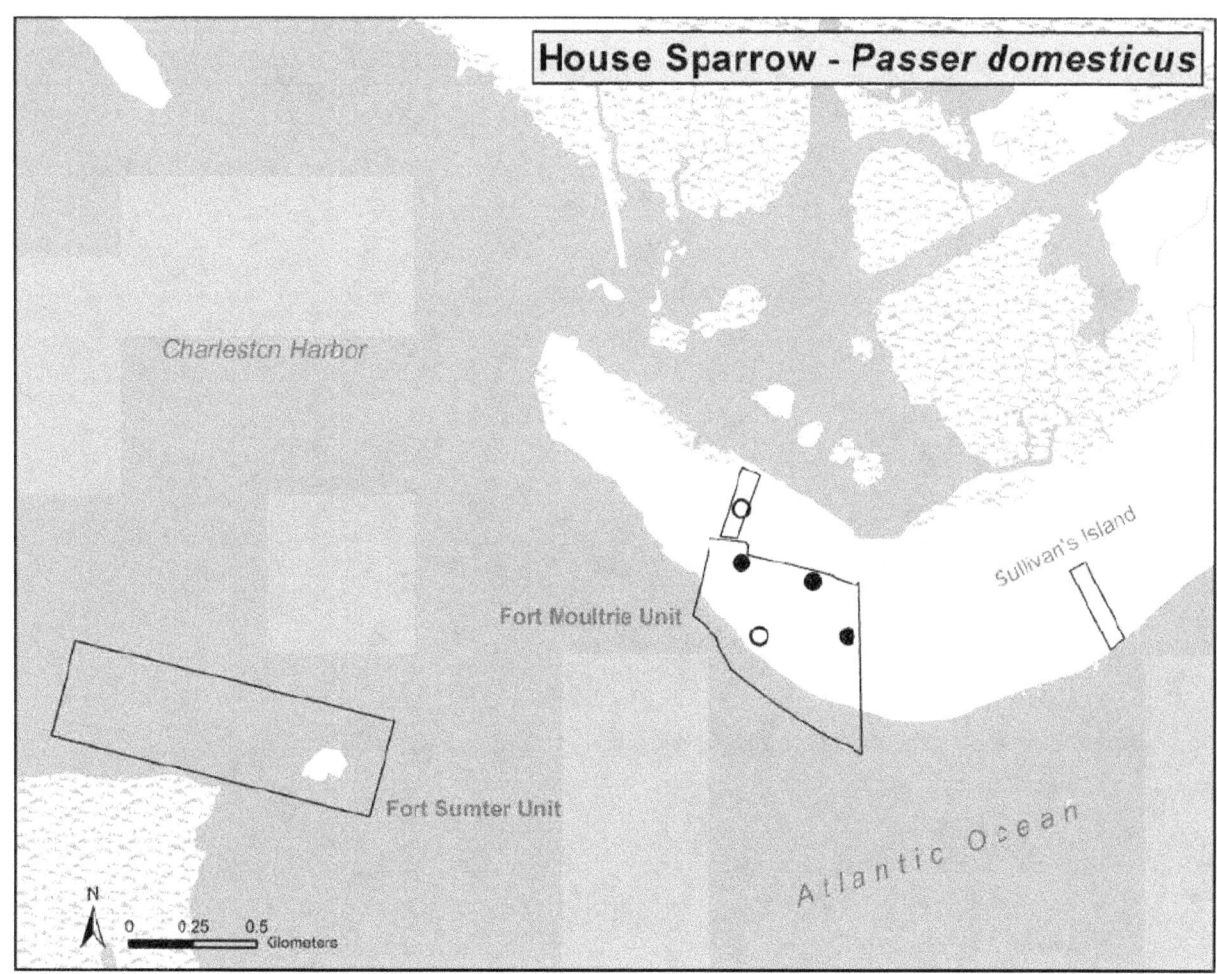

Figure D-20. Sampling locations where House Sparrow (*Pa sser domesti us*) was detected at FOSU, 2010. ● = detected, ○ = not detected.

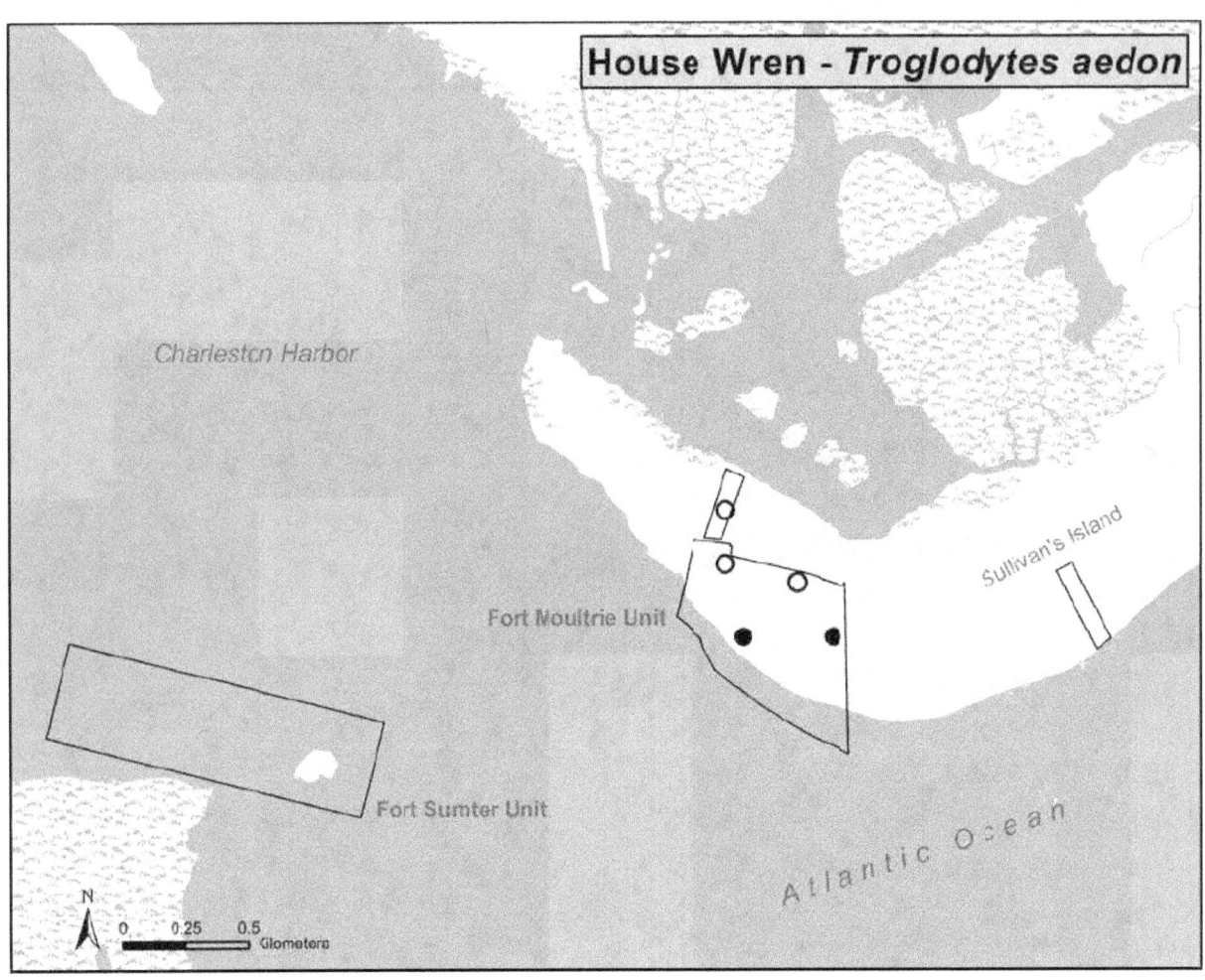

Figure D-21. Sampling locations where House Wren (*Troglodytes aedon*) was detected at FOSU, 2010.
● = detected, ○ = not letected.

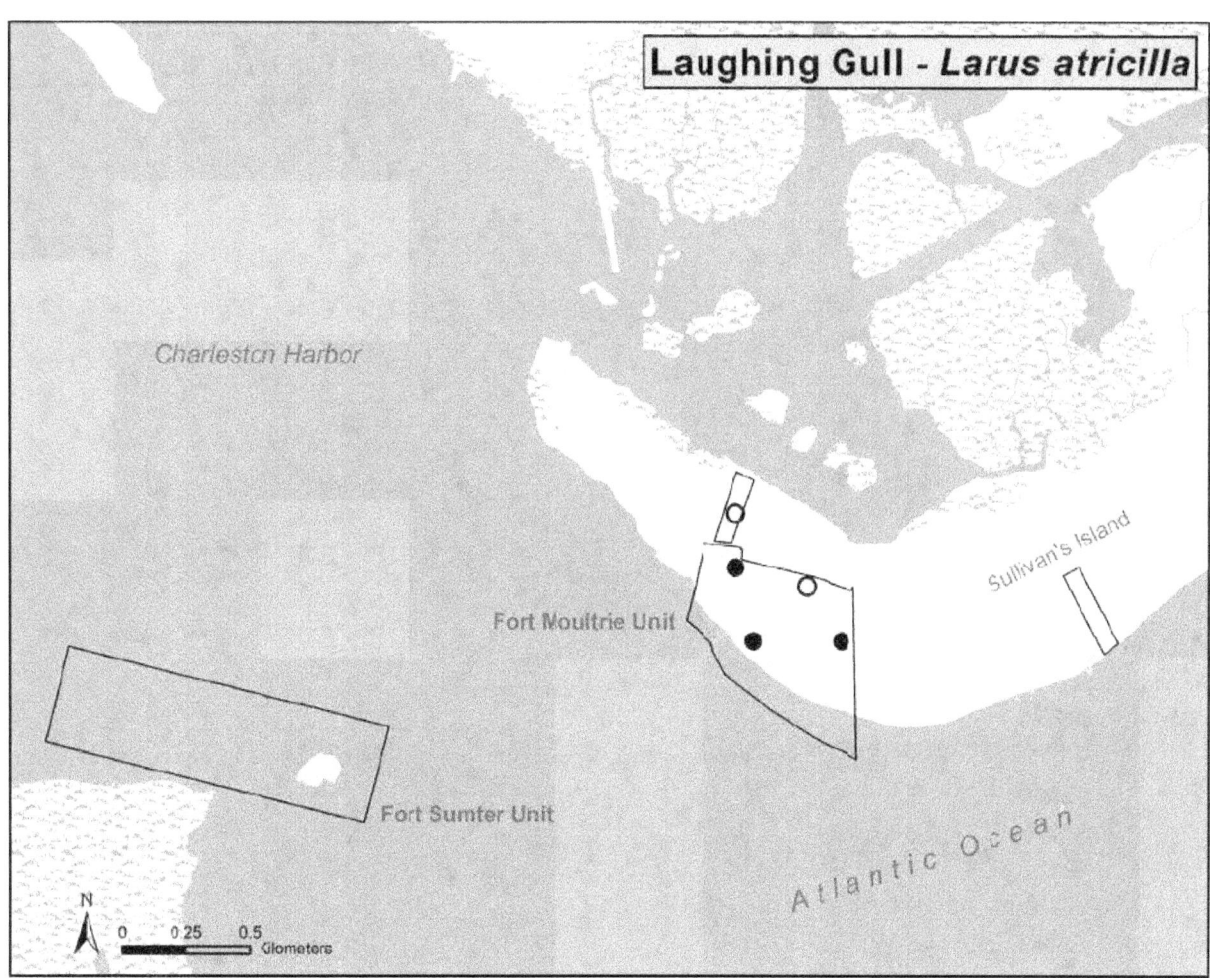

Figure D-22. Sampling locations where Laughing Gull (*Larus atricilla*) was detected at FOSU, 2010. ● = detected, ○ = not detected.

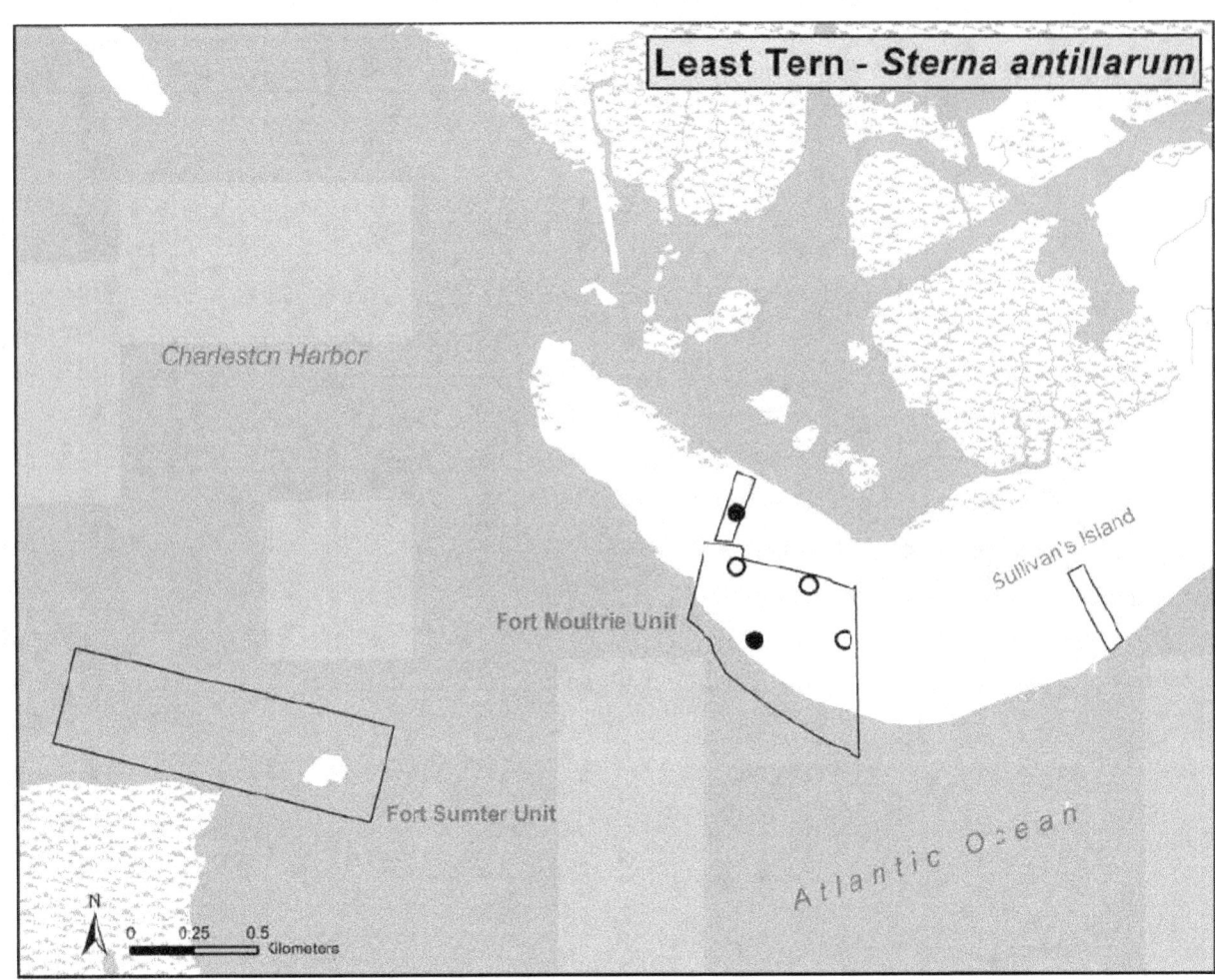

Figure D-23. Sampling locations where Least Tern (*Sterna antillarum*) was detected at FOSU, 2010. ● = detected, ○ = not detected.

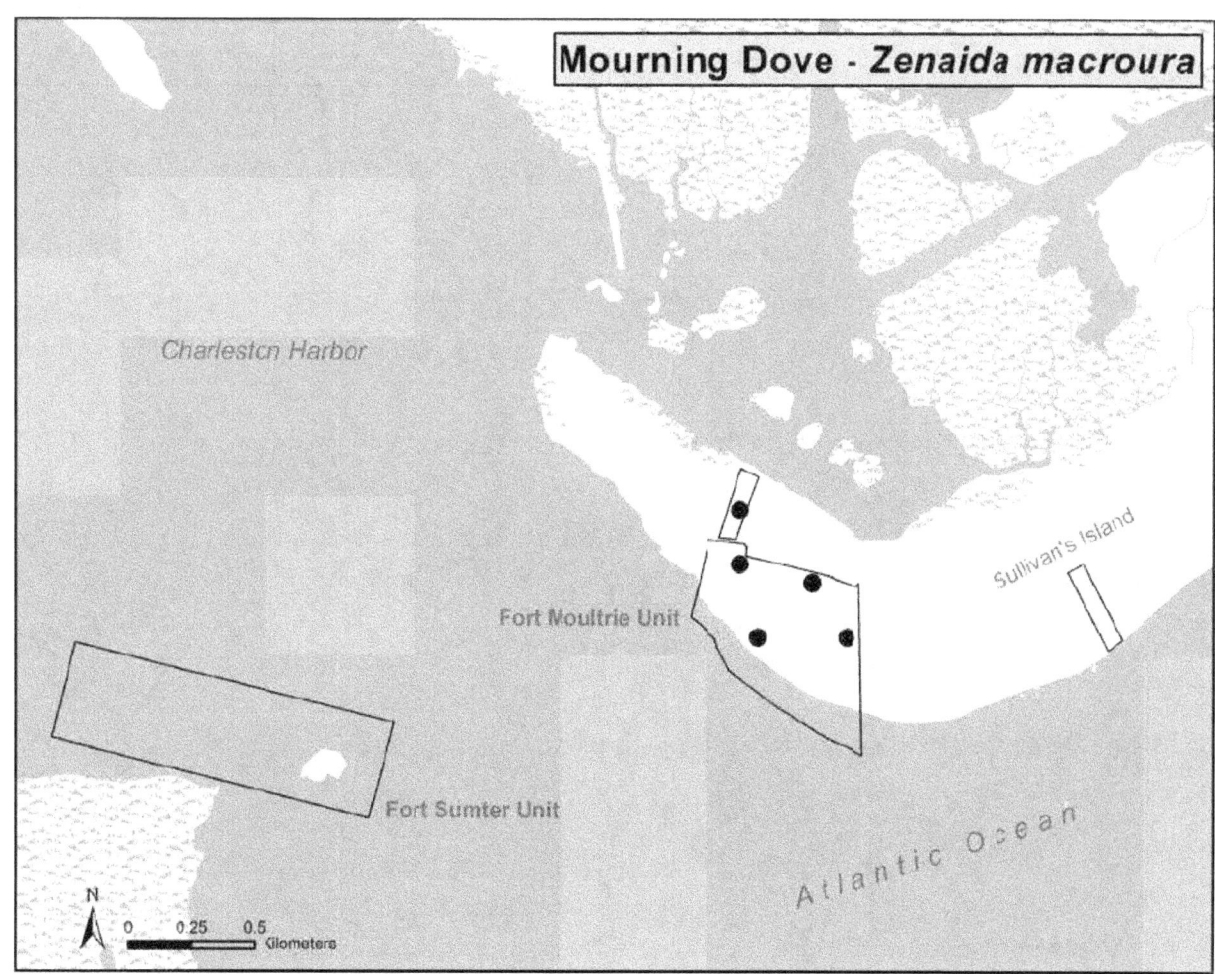

Figure D-24. Sampling locations where Mourning Dove (*Zenaida macroura*) was detected at FOSU, 2010. ● = detected, ○ = not detected.

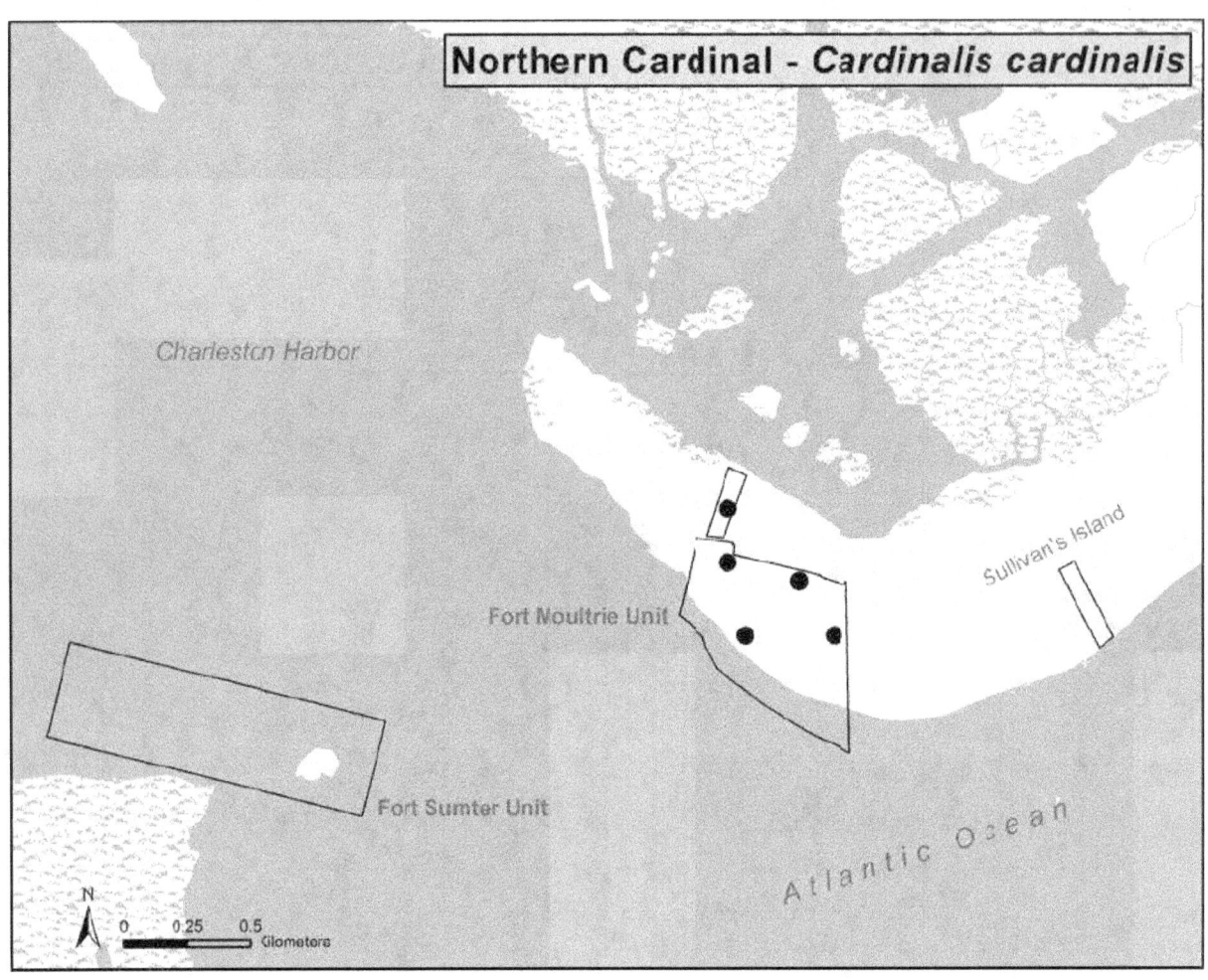

Figure D-25. Sampling locations where Northern Cardinal (*Cardinalis cardinalis*) was detected at FOSU, 2010. ● = detected, ○ = not detected.

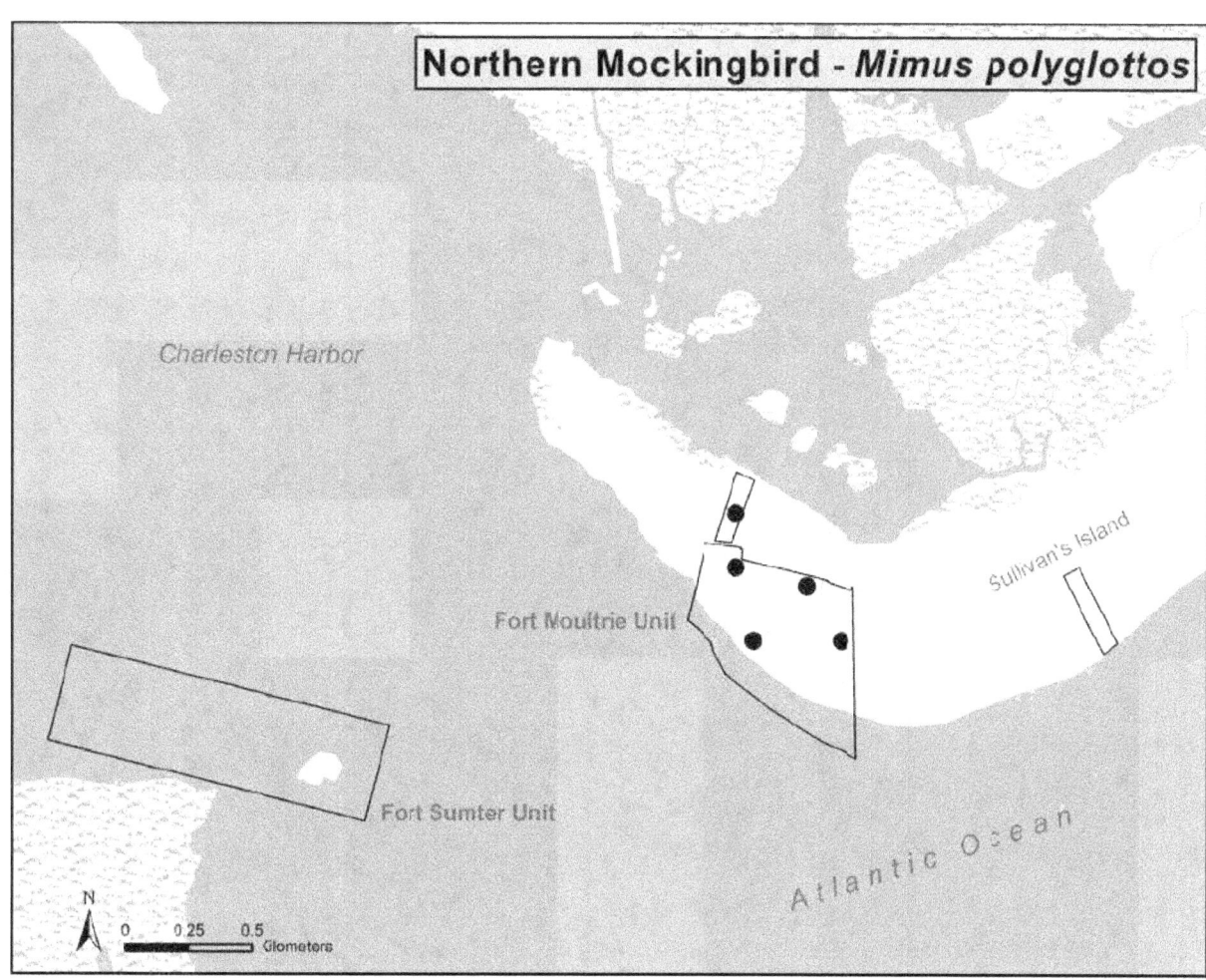

Figure D-26. Sampling locations where Northern Mockingbird (*Mimus polyglottos*) was detected at FOSU, 2)10. • = detected, ○ = not detected.

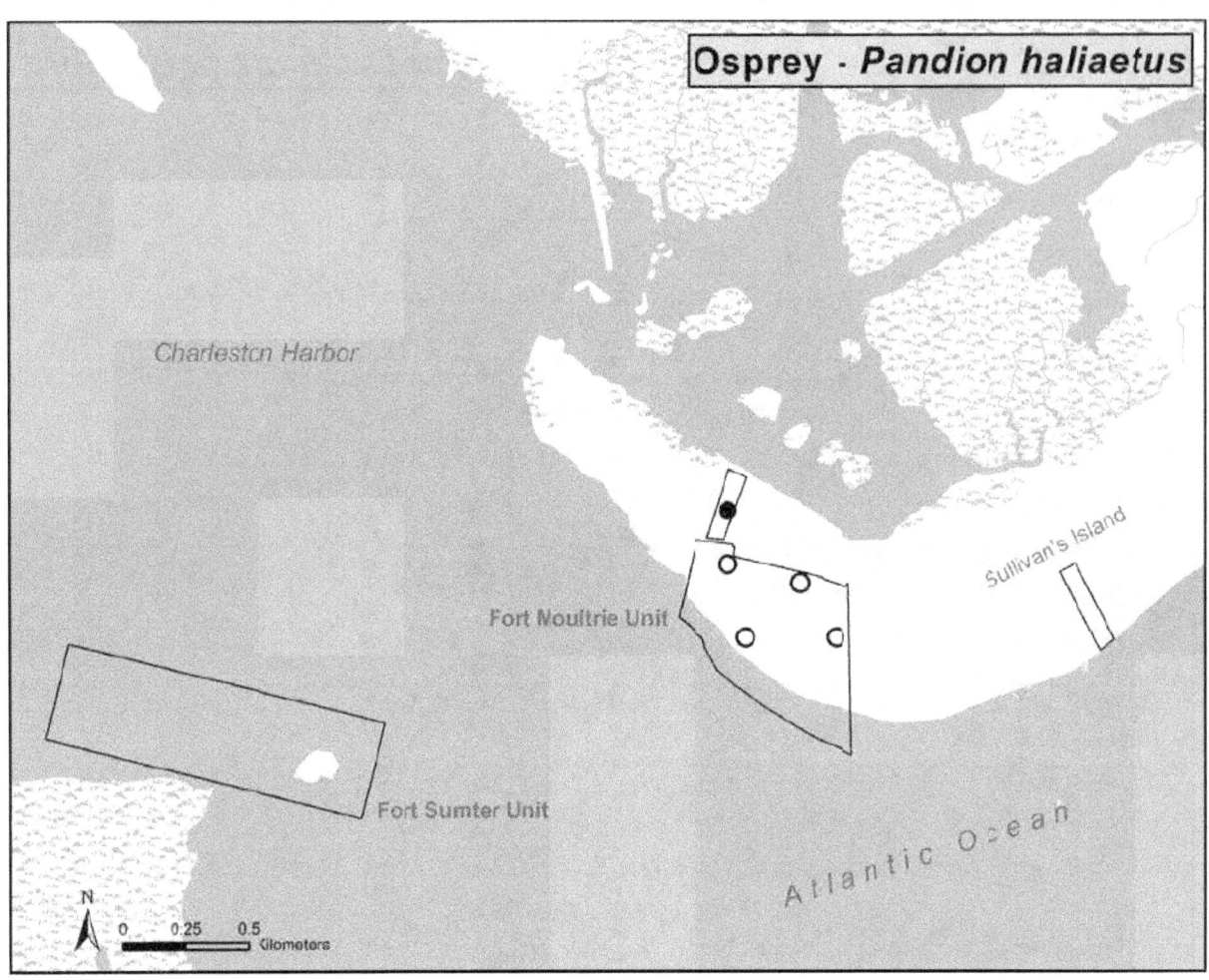

Figure D-27. Sampling locations where Osprey (*Pandion haliaetus*) was detected at FOSU, 2010. ● = detected, ○ = not detected.

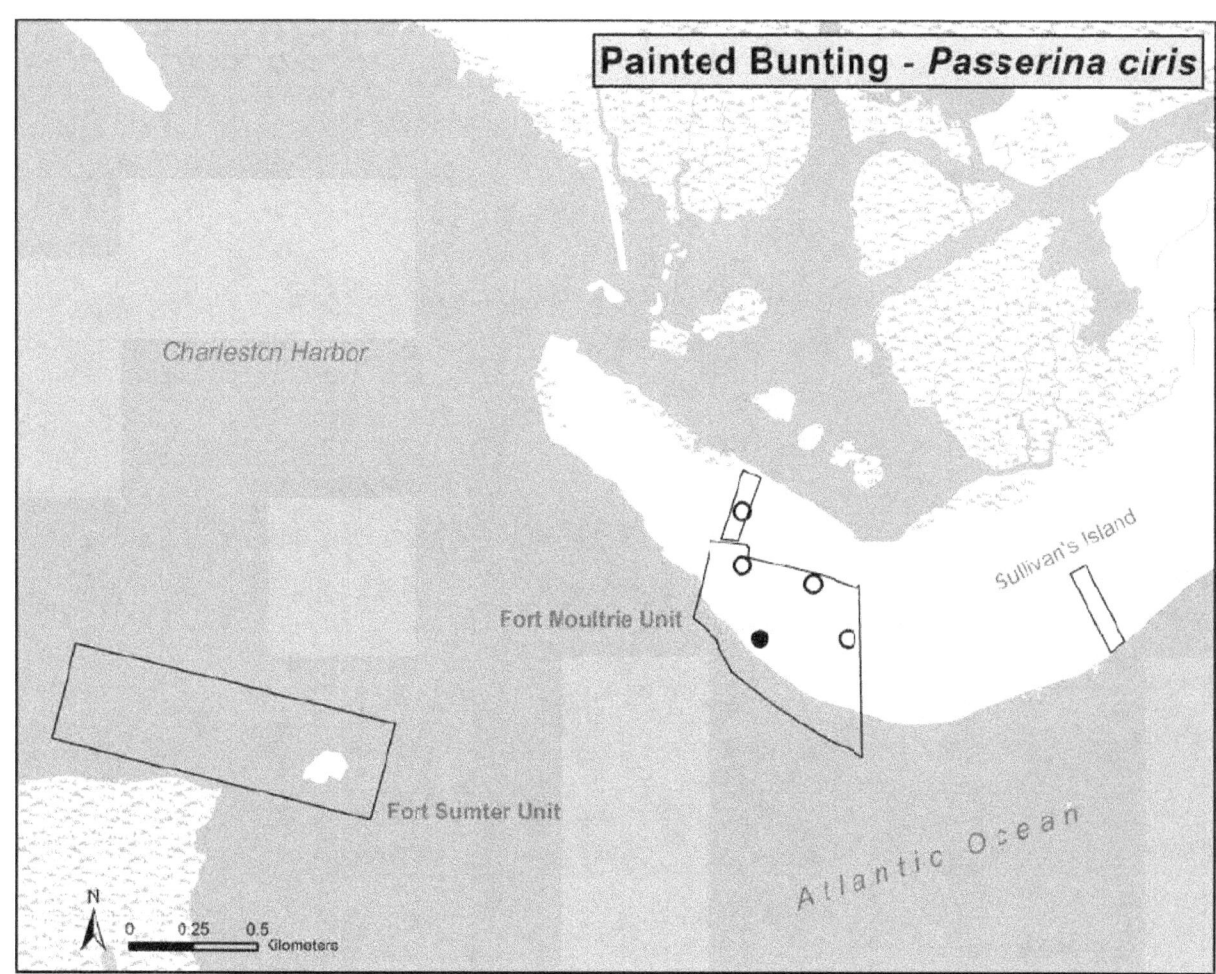

Figure D-28. Sampling locations where Painted Bunting (*Passerina ciris*) was detected at FOSU, 2010. ● = detected, ○ = not detected.

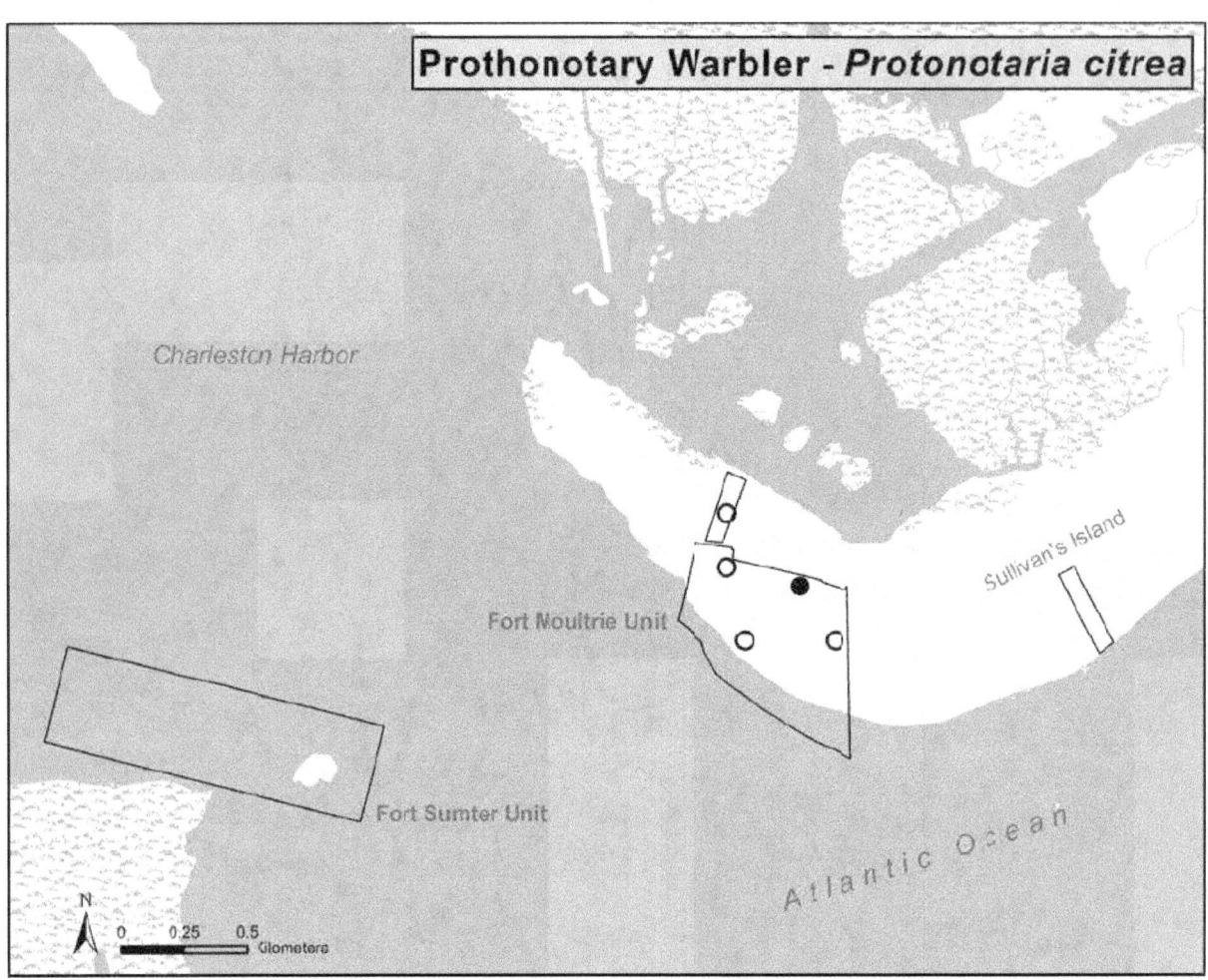

Figure D-29. Sampling locations where Prothonotary Warbl r (*Protonota ia citrea*) was detected at FOSU, 2)10. ● = detected, ○ = not detected.

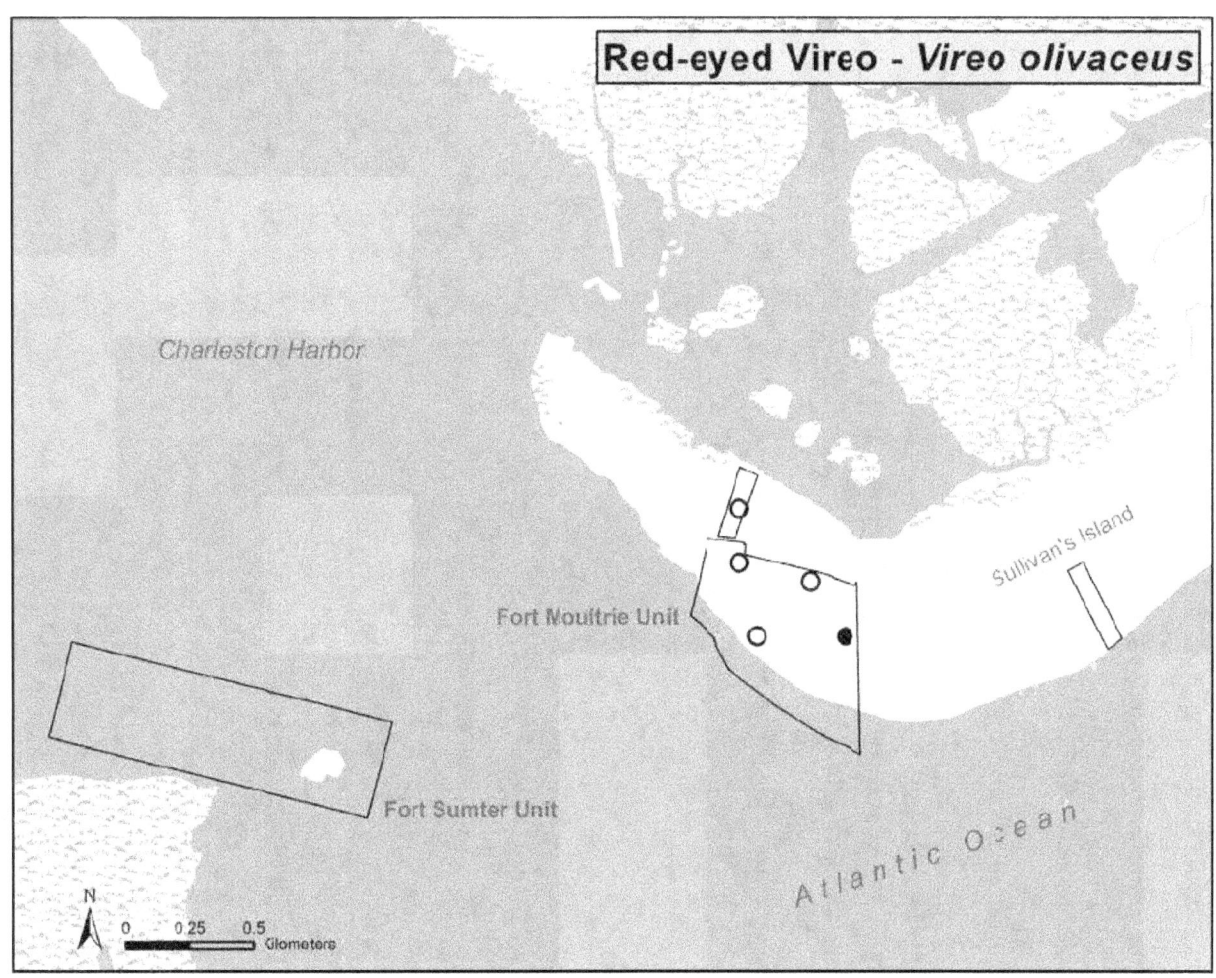

Figure D-30. Sampling locations where Red-eyed Vireo (*Vireo olivaceus*) was detected at FOSU, 2010. ● = detected, ○ = not detected.

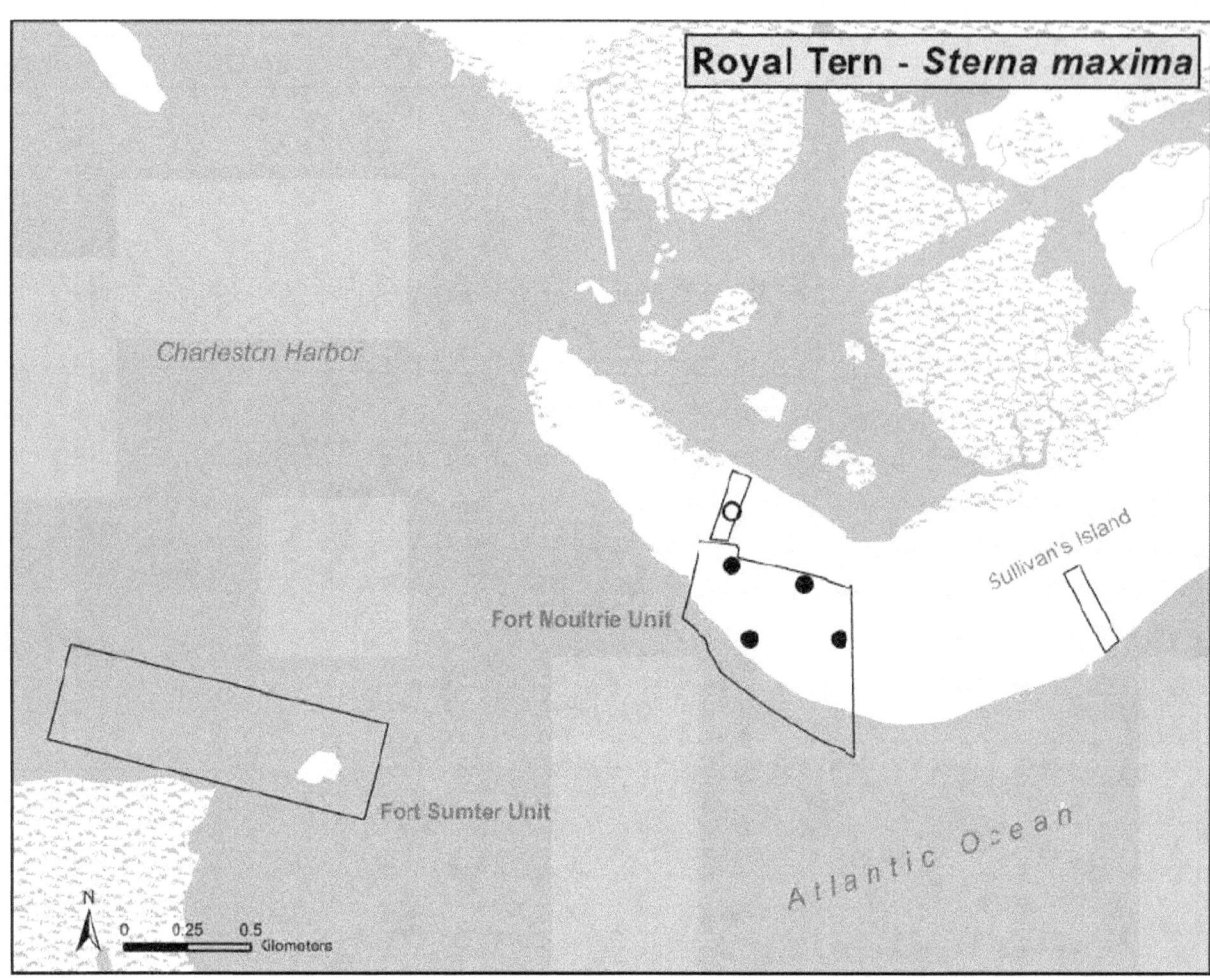

Figure D-31. Sampling locations where Royal Tern (*Sterna naxima*) was detected at FOSU, 2010. ● = detected, ○ = not detected.

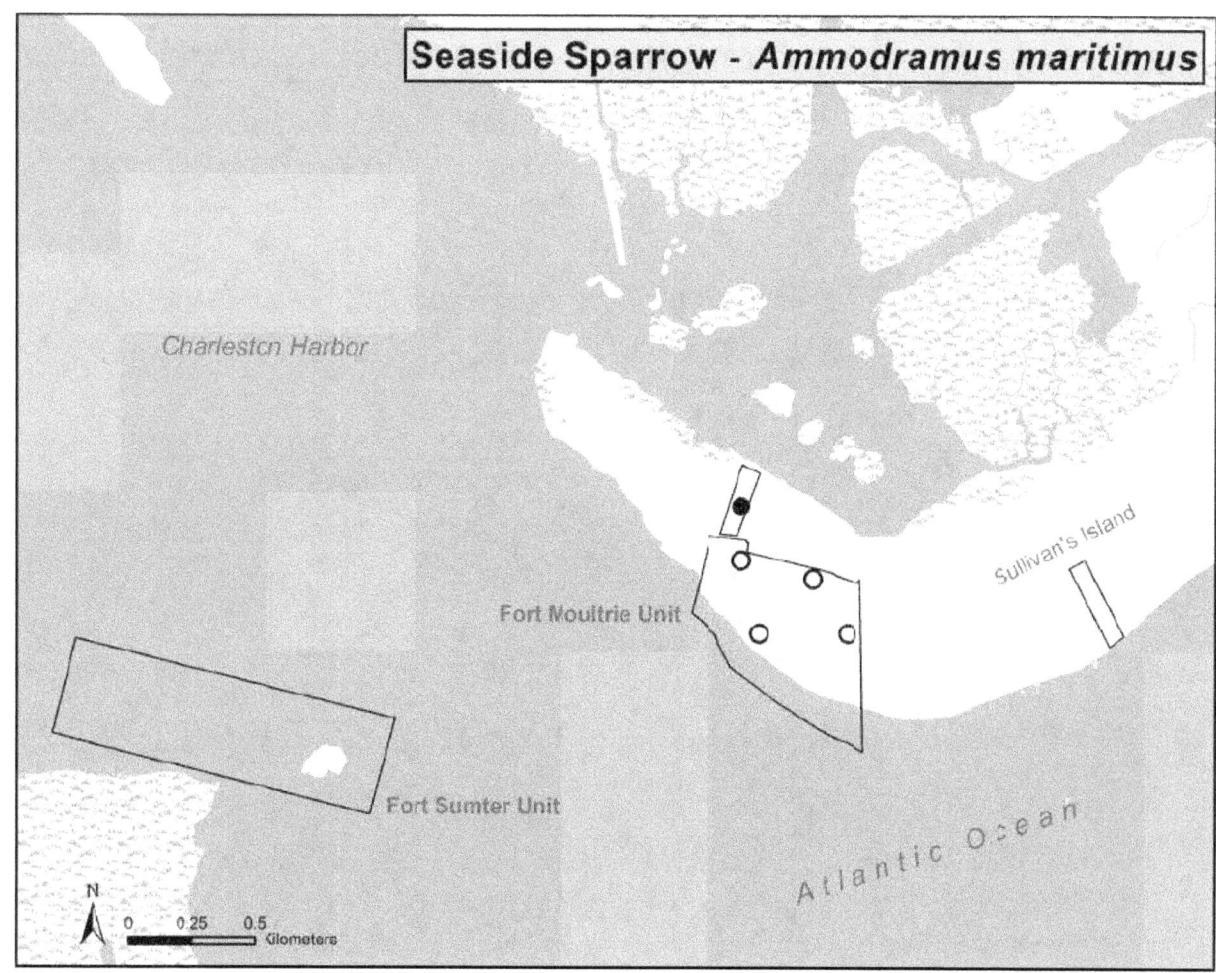

Figure D-32. Sampling locations where Seaside Sparrow (*Ammodramus maritimus*) was detected at FOSU, 2)10. • = detected, ○ = not detected.

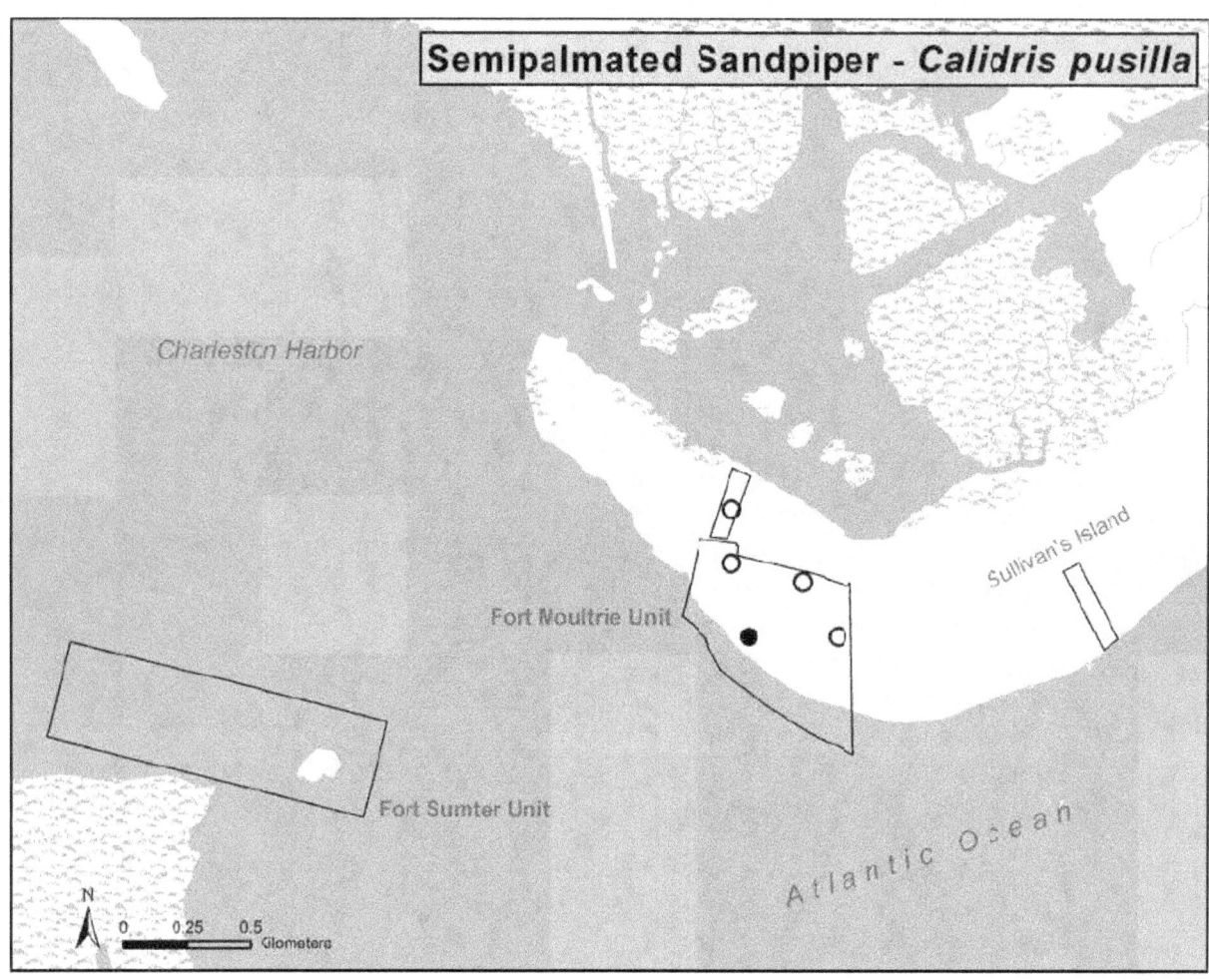

Figure D-33. Sampling locations where Semipalmated Sandpiper (*Calidris pusilla*) was detected at FOSU, 2)10. ● = detected, ○ = not detected.

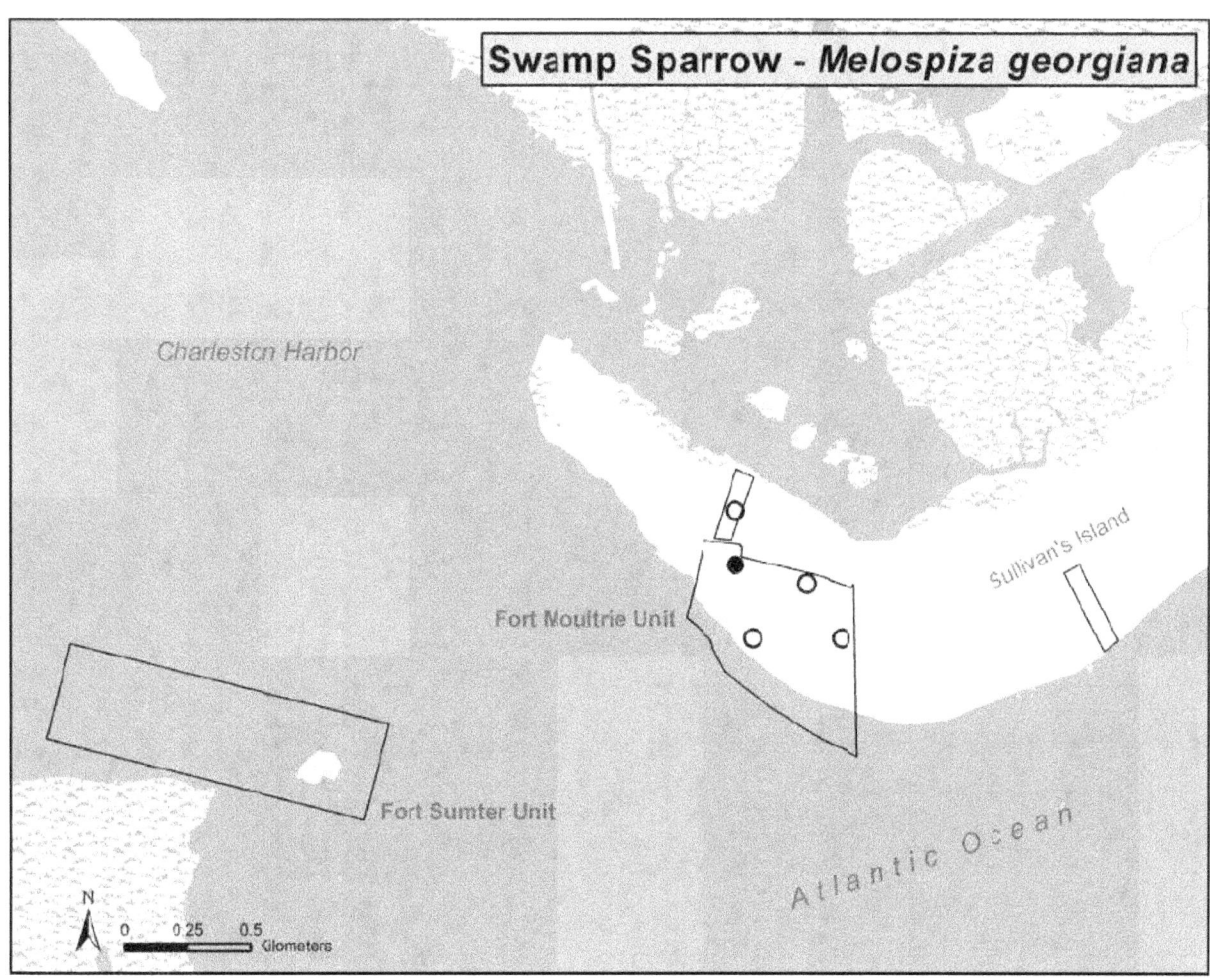

Figure D-34. Sampling locations where Swamp Sparrow (*Melospiza geo giana*) was detected at FOSU, 2010. ● = detected, ○ = not detected.

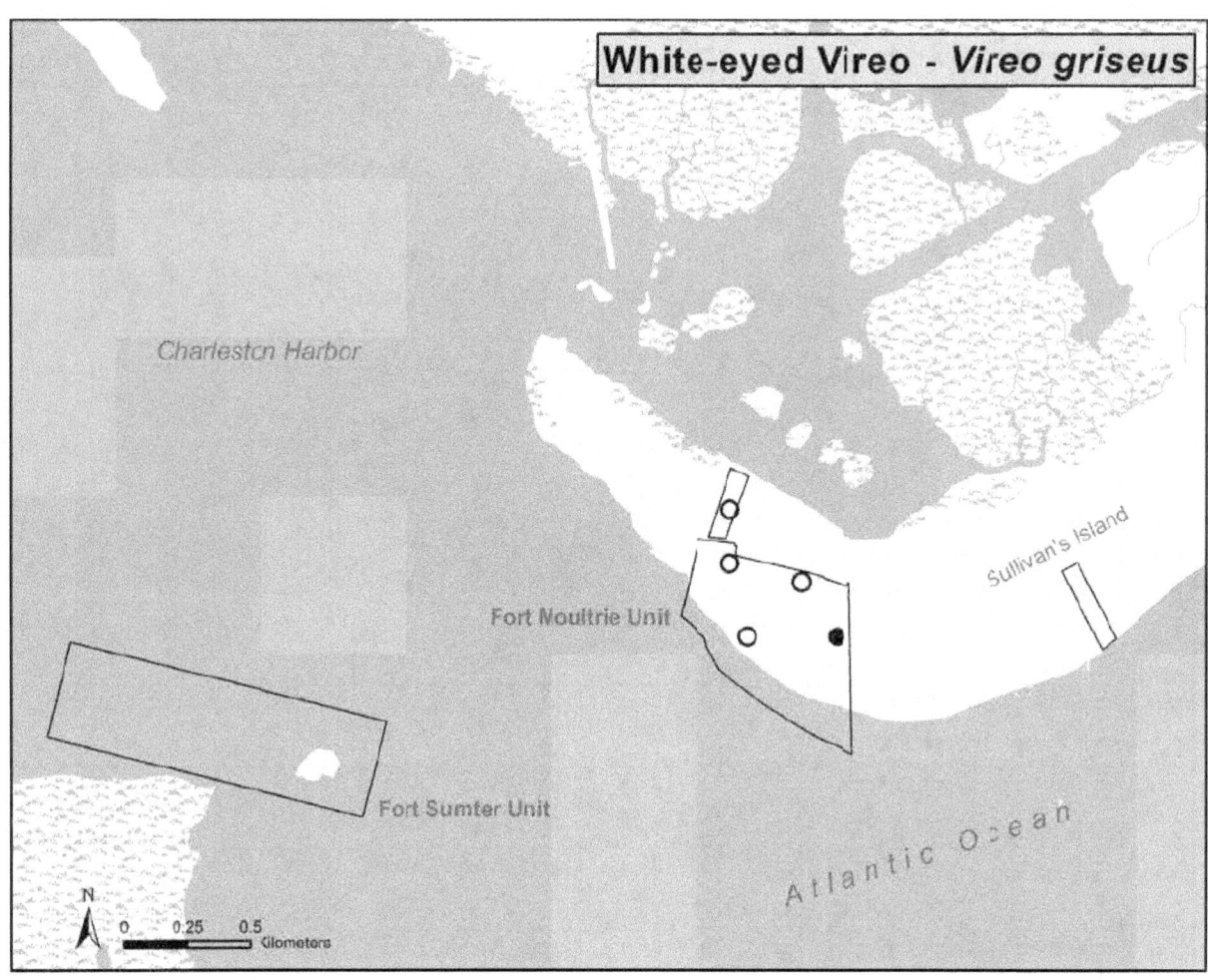

Figure D-35. Sampling locations where White-eyed Vireo (*Vireo griseus*) was detected at FOSU, 2010. ● = detected, ○ = not detected.

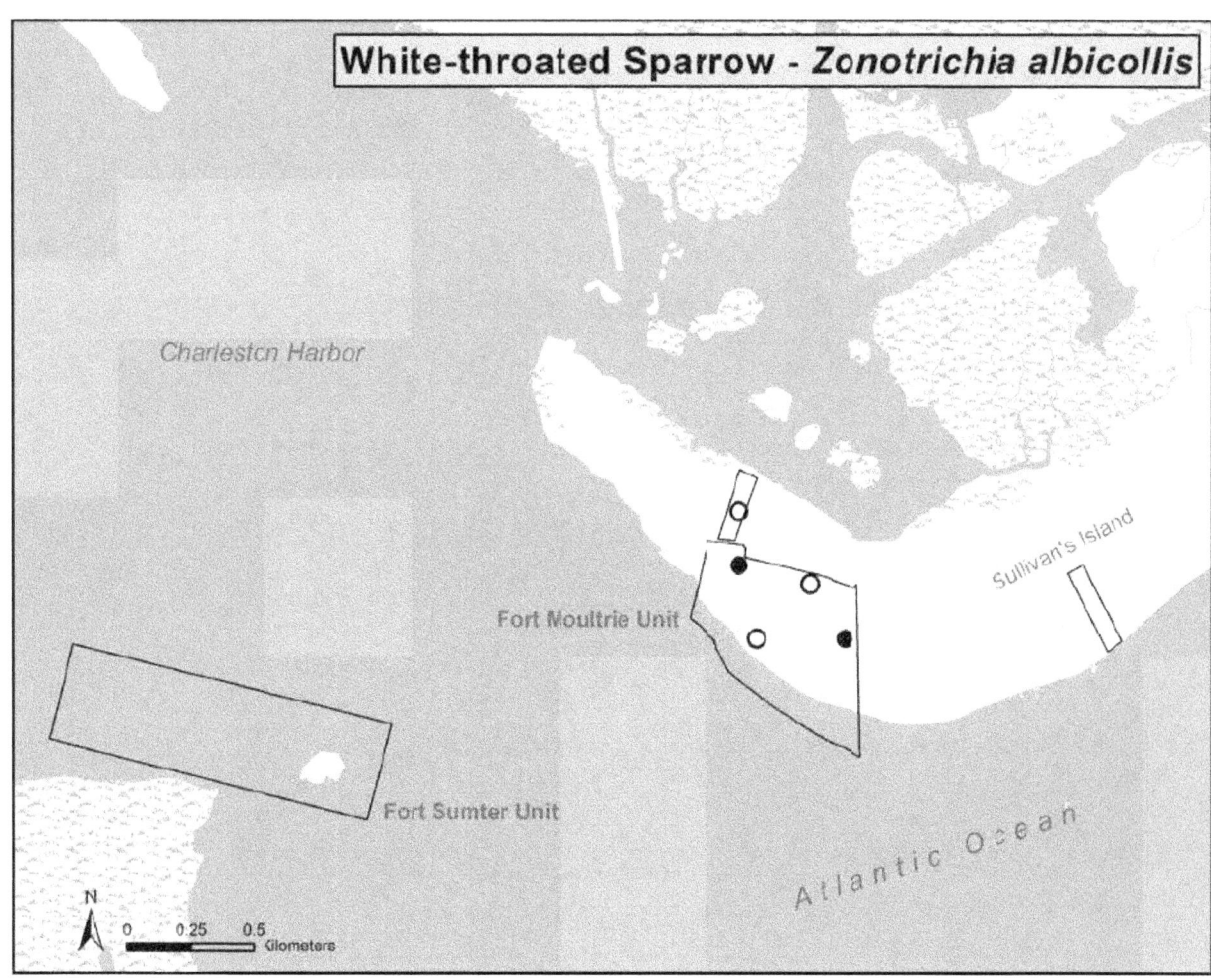

Figure D-36. Sampling locations where White-throated Sparrow (*Zonotri hia albicollis*) was detected at FOSU, 2)10. ● = detected, ○ = not detected.